DECENTRALIZATION PROJECT
FY 1973-74

STUDIES IN WELFARE POLICY

NUMBER 4

DECENTRALIZED DELINQUENCY SERVICES IN MICHIGAN

*Differential Placement and Its Impact on
Program Effectiveness and Cost-Effectiveness*

State of Michigan
Department of Social Services
John Dempsey, Director
Leland Hall, Deputy Director for
Quality Control and Program Analysis
Gerben DeJong, Director, Social Services Evaluation
and Analysis Division

By:

Laurence Max
Thomas Downs

March, 1975

Library of Congress
Catalog Card Number: 75-10233

Publication Number 192 (Revised 3-75)

PREFACE

In 1971 the Michigan Department of Social Services embarked on a program to expand the range of services available to delinquent state wards. The new approach to juvenile justice services revolves around the provision of decentralized services through a broadened network of services ranging from community residential care facilities, such as group homes and halfway houses, to nonresidential attention centers. As part of the growing network of residential care facilities and ancillary services, the Department has restructured its remaining institutional facilities to provide a greater array of special services. The state institutions have introduced special programs for their standard population as well as for the more severely "disturbed" youth. Thus, the Department of Social Services is moving toward a multi-modality juvenile services system aimed at providing troubled youth and their communities with more relevant and effective services. We are witnessing a recognition on the part of state, county, and local officials that the root causes of delinquency--broken families, the disintegration of the urban community, joblessness, etc.--require a greater continuum of services if the delinquency service system is to transcend its well-intended but largely ineffective efforts. To this end, there has been increasing interest and program activity in community based programs.

The report that follows focusses primarily on the Decentralization Project, which might be viewed as a forerunner of a more comprehensive state system. Operating out of Wayne County, the state's most urbanized area, the Decentralization Project represents a model for statewide decentralized youth services. While there have been difficulties in the development and application of the model, the concept has been widely accepted and promises in large part to shape the development of youth services throughout the state.

This study is the second effort to assess the dynamics of the Wayne County youth services system and to determine the relative

iii

effectiveness and cost-effectiveness of community and institutional programs. It is a companion study to the Decentralization Project Year-End Research and Evaluation Report, FY 1972-73. As the sample size expands, the research group intends to provide increasingly rigorous examination of the relative impacts of all of the service modalities incorporated in the Department of Social Services youth services system.

April, 1975   Laurence J. Max
Lansing, Michigan

ACKNOWLEGEMENTS

For their contribution to this report, specific acknowledgements are due to a number of individuals. First, our appreciation to the Statistical Analysis and Evaluation Division, particularly to Robert Lovell, Linda Kohl, Steve Miller, and T. K. Bisht, for their participation in the programming and statistical output for this study. Our thanks also to Barry Goldberg, who acted as liaison with UNCO, Inc., providers of the RCEM proprietary computer software package. The entire study was funded by the Law Enforcement Assistance Administration under the auspices of the Michigan Office of Criminal Justice Programs. The authors are grateful for the cooperation received from the Wayne County Aftercare staff, the Office of Children and Youth Services, and staff of the Decentralization Project.

In the preparation of this study, Thomas Downs was primarily responsible for the collection of outcome and cost data, the demographic analysis presented in the appendices, and the attention center analysis in Chapter 5. Laurence Max was responsible for the design and execution of the study and the preparation of the remaining chapters. The authors wish to thank Alvin Horn, Diane Ball, and the Maxey institutional staff for their cooperation in the analysis of the institutional and community components in Chapter 4, and especially Deborah Williams for her painstaking assistance in processing the raw data for this study.

Marguerite Damer, who carefully and capably typed the final draft of this study, deserves special credit. Finally, the authors acknowledge with appreciation the invaluable critical review of the substance and organization of the study provided by Gerben DeJong, Director of the Social Services Evaluation and Analysis Division.

Laurence J. Max
Thomas B. Downs

SUMMARY OF MAJOR FINDINGS [1]

The concept of decentralized delinquency services and planned differential placement have been subjected to critical analysis to determine the extent and effectiveness of their application in the Decentralization Project. To establish an analytic framework, the client population was assessed on key variables and the following profile emerged:

1. The Wayne County delinquent state ward population is predominantly black and predominantly male. Approximately 60 percent of the population is black and about 75 percent is male. (Appendix B-1.)

2. About 55 percent of the Wayne County delinquent state ward population are considered to be aggressive and 45 percent are considered to be nonaggressive. Most nonaggressive youth are status offenders. (Appendix B-2.)

3. Some 85 percent of all females in the population were classified as nonaggressive while only 33 percent of all males were labeled as nonaggressive. (Appendix B-2.1.)

4. Black youth are more likely to have aggressive offense histories (62 percent) than white youth (35 percent). (Appendix B-2.2.)

5. The state juvenile services system is quicker to intervene in the lives of white, female, nonaggressive youth than in the delinquent careers of black, male, aggressive youth once an offense has been committed. (Appendix B-5.6.)

Although the client population is notably heterogeneous, the intake and placement making system exercises considerable discrimination, with respect to client characteristics and offense histories, in the selective channelization of youth into their eventual first placements:

---

[1] A more abstract summary of conclusions and policy implications can be found in Chapter 6, pp. 79-85.

6. The Wayne County Court secures placement for about 11 percent of the youth they commit to the state. They place mainly white nonaggressive males, and place all but a few of these youth in private institutions. (Section 3.3.1.)

7. The Intake Center places a contrasting group of mainly black aggressive males and places about half of these youth in the community and half in state institutions. Although the Intake Center works with the most difficult-to-place subpopulation, the Center diverts more state wards from institutions than does the Wayne County Court or the intake staff located in the Youth Home. (Section 3.3.3.)

8. Although the placement-making system is achieving a larger measure of differential placement, too many nonaggressive youth (primarily status offenders) continue to be placed in institutions largely due to the Wayne County Court's policy of placing nearly all of its nonaggressive youth in private institutions. (Section 3.4.3.)

9. To date, attitudinal measures fail to fully support the position that institutionally placed youth are more "delinquent" or more "disturbed" than their community placed counterparts. (Section 3.4.4.)

In addition to the differentiated intake procedure, the project offers a variety of placement options. The Decentralization Project includes an institutional component at Maxey Boys' Training School which provides ostensibly effective intensive treatment for selected youth. In addition, it includes community residential care components in Wayne County and community-based attention center programs in Wayne and Muskegon counties and, prior to its closure, in Berrien County. Goal attainment analysis of the community-based facilities indicates that:

10. Wayne County's state-operated community residential care facilities compare favorably with outstate facilities except with respect to a youth's release status. Between a third and one-half of all youth were not released satisfactorily, suggesting that behavior goals had not been attained. Moreover, the Defer House has a particularly high truancy rate (44 percent) which combined with other adverse anecdotal information requires further investigation. (Section 4.1.2.)

11. Both Wayne County attention centers serve a large number of module 5 youth who are only a few months away from discharge. The level of programming for these youth, however necessary, is too elementary and remedial to adequately prepare youth for independent living. (Sections 4.2.1.2, 4.2.1.3, and 4.2.1.5.)

12. The Wayne County attention centers appear to have some impact on reducing the incidence of delinquency in areas immediately surrounding the attention centers. The magnitude of this impact is unknown. (Section 4.2.1.4.)

13. The decision to close the Berrien County Attention Center was justified. Because of initiatives taken by the local community to divert youth from the juvenile justice system, the Attention Center was destined to serve an ever decreasing number of state wards. (Section 4.2.2.)

The relative effectiveness analysis indicates that the type of intake procedure a youth is referred to influences the efficacy of his eventual first-placement:

14. Despite the fact that the Intake Center is placing more serious offenders, placements made by the Intake Center are generally more effective and cost-effective than placements made for state wards by the Wayne County Court or by the intake staff located in the Youth Home. (Section 5.1.)

15. Male youth with longer lengths of stay in the Intake Center achieve more effective and cost-effective outcomes than those placed by the court or those placed directly out of the Youth Home. (Section 5.1.)

16. The Defer House as an intake facility appears to have a deteriorating impact upon the females residing there as noted by the decreasing effectiveness ratios for increasing lengths of stay and by the high truancy rate. (Section 5.2.)

17. The Intake Center is most instrumental in enabling aggressive hard-to-place youth obtain less structured and non-institutional placements which are at least as effective and a bit more cost-effective than placements made by intake staff in the Youth Home. (Section 5.2.)

The relative effectiveness and cost-effectiveness study also suggests that community-based alternatives to institutionalization of

ix

delinquent youth have been relatively effective in achieving positive outcomes during placement.

18. Although institutions were found to be slightly more effective than community placements, the higher cost of institutions make institutional care far less cost-effective than community care.[2]

19. Success in initial placement appears to be strongly correlated with the seriousness of the youth's offense. More aggressive youth appear to do better regardless of initial placement or the intake process through which a youth was channeled. (Sections 5.2 and 5.5.)

20. Younger and less aggressive youth who are admitted early to the juvenile justice system achieve less effective outcomes than do their older counterparts. This finding suggests that early adjudication does not allow the marginally delinquent youth sufficient time to correct his behavior through self-adjustment. (Section 5.6.)

21. Youth who are adjudicated between one and two years from the time of their first offense achieved more effective and cost-effective results than youth who were adjudicated much earlier or much later. (Sections 5.7 and 5.8.)

---

[2]The institutions' greater effectiveness can in large part be attributed to the compulsory participation in skill attainment programs. Skill attainment was one of the measures used to determine effectiveness.

The Implications of Research Findings

The research findings are generally supportive of the position that, for most youth, community placement is at least as effective as incarceration as a short-run deterrent to recidivism and as a facilitator of educational and skill training objectives. There is evidence that suggests, inconclusively, that this pattern of effectiveness persists after release from placement.

Differential treatment, such as it exists, has been shown to be a viable concept, although the evidence to date suggests that high aggressiveness is not necessarily the only parameter for appropriate placement in institutional settings. All other factors held equal, the institution is probably best suited for the retention of chronically truant youth or youth with severe lack of controls who also have aggressive offense histories. There is evidence that the institutional setting is especially conducive to positive outcomes among youth with the most aggressive histories. (Tables 5.5.1, 5.5.2)

TABLE OF CONTENTS

APPENDICES

LIST OF TABLES

                              xviii

LIST OF FIGURES

APPENDIX FIGURES

CHAPTER 1

INTRODUCTION

The Decentralization Project is a delinquency services program which began in April 1971 in Wayne County, Michigan and had, as its central goal, the provision of a "range of community placement and treatment alternatives as a means of preventing the indiscriminate use of institutions."[1] Discriminate utilization of placement and treatment alternatives was to be achieved through the use of planned differential placement, whereby each delinquent youth is recognized as unique and receives placement and treatment consistent with his or her needs.

The fiscal year 1972-73 evaluation of the project demonstrated that decentralization had contributed to a 35 percent decrease in institutional placements, and had provided more effective and substantially more cost-effective placements for the majority of community placed youth. The past fiscal year culminated in the commitment of state funds to the project and tacit approval of the decentralization philosophy.

The Decentralization components that this report directly addresses include the Intake Center modality (which at the time of this study was shifting from a single unit, the Townsend Center, to a two-center system), the attention center modality, the community residential care modality, and the institutional components.

1.1   Intake Services

The Intake Center was originally designed as a short-term (10-day) diagnostic facility, to be utilized for the development of a specialized treatment plan for each youth, which could draw on expanded community resources for placement and services. The Intake Center was to facilitate the delivery of decentralized services (e.g., community

---

[1] 1973-74 Grant Application

1

residential care) by providing careful preplacement diagnostics to
determine which youth were best suited for community care, institutional
care, or other services.

In evaluating the intake process, we will be addressing a
number of concerns:

(1) What factors contribute to the decision process that
determine the nature and location of intake services?

(2) What youth characteristics are most represented in each
of the intake populations?

(3) What factors lead to the eventual determination of first
placement?

This report will explore the nature of the intake process
starting with the Wayne County Juvenile Court which not only adjudicates,
but, in many instances, also places a youth prior to committing him to
state wardship. Those state wards not placed by the court are screened
by Department of Social Services intake staff located in the county
youth home for placement or transfer to the Intake Center for further
evaluation and treatment prior to final placement. In short, we will
examine the extent to which the intake process selects youth for Intake
Center services and the function of the Intake Center as an interim
placement for especially difficult-to-place youth.

1.2   Attention Center Services

The attention centers are "nonresidential multi-purpose
centers, located among high delinquency populations...," designed to
(1) "program wards away from further deviance," and (2) "guide the
community to better cope with its problems." The project operates
three[2] nonresidential centers serving approximately 30-60
wards and provides ancillary services to the entire youth community and
their families. The centers operate five to six days a week, 12 to 14

---

[2]The fourth facility, in Benton Harbor, has been closed. This
will be discussed more fully in Chapter 4, Section 4.2.2.

hours a day on a flexible schedule. The target ward population is designated as low-risk youth who need structure not available from their families. There is considerable evidence that the actual ward population is, despite these criteria, highly intractable and represents the most "marginal" of the community placed youth -- youth for whom educational and skill programs in more traditional facilities such as public schools and institutions are demonstrably not feasible.

This report will address:

(1) The nature of the attention center population;

(2) The interaction of the attention centers with the Intake Center;

(3) The effects of the attention center on the surrounding community, and

(4) The appropriateness of the attention centers as treatment alternatives.

1.3 Community Residential Care Services

The community residential care modality includes, as part of the Wayne County Family and Youth Services System, four group homes and two halfway houses. The target populations for both modalities include youth for whom community placement is considered more appropriate than institutional care. This population falls into two groups: (1) those for whom community residential care or other community placement is the first placement as a state ward (module 3 youth), and (2) those who have previously been institutionalized and are returning to community placements (module 5 youth). The group homes serve predominantly module 3 youth, the halfway houses predominantly module 5. One of the group homes, the Defer Home, serves as a short-term intake and diagnostic facility for female wards.

Community nonresidential care usually includes wards on independent living status, receiving foster care, or living with relatives or parents. For purposes of this analysis these groups are included, with community residential care, in the category labeled "community placement."

1.4   Institutional Services

Wayne County state wards receiving institutional services may
be placed in one of two general types of institutions: (1) public institutions such as the W. J. Maxey Boys' Training School and the Adrian
Training School, or (2) private institutions whose services are available on a purchase-of-services basis.   Some 36 percent of all Wayne
County institutional placements are made with private providers.   These
placements represent 25 percent of all Wayne County state ward placements.

The various intake services made possible by the Decentraliza-
tion Project have reduced the need for extensive evaluation and diag-
nostic services at the Reception Center located at the Maxey Training
School.   This reduced load has resulted in a reorganization of the
Reception Center to include two specialized programs: (1) an Intensive
Treatment Program for serious behavior-problem youth, and (2) a Crisis
Intervention and Reevaluation Unit for youth referred from other units
in the institution for crisis management or reevaluation.

For purposes of a comparative analysis, this report will con-
sider all institutional services and all community services as two di-
chotomous groups of services.   The report will focus on:

(1)   The relative-effectiveness and cost-effectiveness of
      community vs. institutional services; and

(2)   The degree to which the institutional components of
      Decentralization have met their goals.

1.5   Scope of this Report

This report will examine the Wayne County system of decentral-
ized youth services at each level of the system.   Chapter 3 and Appendix
B assesses the characteristics of the delinquent youth population.
Particular emphasis is placed upon the interaction of client variables.
In Chapter 3 we fully examine the intake and placement process, and the
effects of each on the phenomenon of planned differential placement.

In Chapter 4 each of the major placement categories and the attention centers are assessed on the basis of project goal attainment measures. Chapter 5 presents an analysis of the relative effectiveness and relative cost-effectiveness of community and institutional services for categories of youth aligned by critical demographic and offense characteristics. Effectiveness and cost-effectiveness is examined at the third and sixth month after placement.

In the next chapter, a detailed description of the research methodology and analytic framework employed in this study is described.

CHAPTER 2

METHODOLOGY

2.1   Data Files

2.1.1   The Demographic File

In order to build a body of data suitable for analysis, we constructed a series of files which became the source of all information needed to evaluate aggregate and case level performance of various program components. Characterizations of individual youth according to offense history, adjudication history, and personal attributes became part of the Demographic File. Essential background information for this file was derived from case file documents, particularly the Initial Social Study, and specific data elements made available from the Child Care Placement Information System. For a description of the Demographic File, see Table 2.1.1.

TABLE 2.1.1

DESCRIPTION OF DEMOGRAPHIC FILE

Number	Item
1	Name
2	Recipient I.D.
3	Date of Birth (D.O.B.)
4	Sex
5	Race
6	Date of admission
7	Load number
8	Age at first recorded offense
9	Age at DSS admission
10	Offense classification
11	Initial placement

The demographic file data was cross-tabulated for the entire sample population, which consists of 416 youth for whom complete records were available. This cross-tabulation is the basis of the analysis of the characteristics of the delinquent state ward in

Chapter 3.

2.1.2   The Quarterly Report File

The basic data retrieval instrument for ongoing monitoring is the Decentralization Quarterly Report. The form is filled out on a quarterly basis by aftercare staff and in many instances is supplemented by information culled from case files in the training schools, camps, or private institutions. The Quarterly Report File is an aggregation of educational, vocational, employment-related and recidivism-related data as reported in the ongoing quarterly data collection process. (A copy of the quarterly report form can be found in Appendix A.)

2.2   The Outcome Scales

The Quarterly Report was the source for outcome data, and forms the basis for the assignment of a combined outcome score, which represents the weighted ranking of each youth on various outcome variables: education, employment/vocational training, recidivism and change-in-placement. The outcome scales form the basis for the relative effectiveness analysis and cost-effectiveness analysis in Chapter 5.

The Outcome Variables:

a.   Education -- The youth's current status with regard to education was noted from quarterly case records. Each educational outcome was coded and assigned a positive, neutral, or negative value as follows:

Code		Value
1	No participation	-
2	Began program	+
3	Completed program	+
4	Terminated unsuccessfully	-
5	Terminated due to placement change	0
6	Continued program with satisfactory progress	+
7	Continued program with unsatisfactory progress	0

b. <u>Employment or Vocational Training</u> -- A single value was extracted from the reported outcomes on the employment or vocational records. Employment records were searched first; if blank, neutral, or negative outcomes were found, the vocational record was searched. In this way the youth was credited for the better of the two associated outcomes.

c. <u>Police Contacts, Truancy, and Arrests</u> -- From the 72 possible patterns or combinations of outcomes in the police contact, truancy, and arrest scales, a scale of 1-13 was developed to account for increasing levels of seriousness of offense. The scale runs from 1 (no truancy, arrest or police contacts) through 13 (aggressive acts on person). In outcomes 6-13, aggressive offenses take precedence over truancies and lesser offenses; thus, a youth cited for lesser offenses as well as an aggressive act on a person is ranked the same as a youth cited only for aggressive offenses.

d. <u>Change-of-Placement</u> -- The placement change outcome scale is predicated on the position that youth who undergo placement changes during their first placement are being subjected to decisions reflecting the system's dynamic response to a perceived inappropriateness of the initial placement. The ranking of the outcome of the placement change depends upon the direction of the placement change, i.e., if the youth was moved to a less structured placement, he received a positive outcome; a more structured placement led to a negative outcome. The outcomes were ranked on a five-point scale, with three representing a neutral (or no change) change in placement.

2.3 <u>The Combined Outcome Scale -- Principle Component Analysis</u>[1]

A central problem in a cost-effectiveness study of youth

---

[1]For a detailed discussion of the principle component analysis, see Appendix A.

placement is obtaining one single index reflecting the youth's "outcome." The choice of a single observable variable, for instance "educational attainment," ignores other important variables, such as "police contacts." Each of the four variables outlined above were assigned weights:

Educational outcome ------------ .2224

Skill attainment -------------- .2992

Police-truancy outcome --------- .8089

Placement outcome ------------- .4547

These weights were then mathematically combined to generate a single outcome (0) score for each youth.

When the outcomes were computed for each of the outcome scale combinations, the resulting distribution of outcomes were grouped roughly into nine classes: 1-9 in order of decreasing social utility. These nine classes represent the final Combined Outcome Scale. Youth in each class can be considered equivalent to each other in terms of the overall "social utility" of their behavior as determined by the principle component analysis.

2.4   Offense Class---Level of Aggressiveness Scale

The Offense Class Scale was generated as one of the principle independent variables. With minor modification, the scale was adapted from the "Target of Aggressiveness" measure developed for an earlier study.

Initial Social Studies (ISS's) were analyzed to determine pre-adjudication offense history. The juvenile offense patterns were categorized subjectively into one of the six offense classes; in each case, the most severe offense tended to determine the offense class, particularly when the offense history included the full range of lesser offenses. The rankings were performed by one researcher trained in the offense classification and use of the scale. These rankings were then checked by the principle researcher for consistency and accuracy. The classes were broad enough to allow a relatively un-ambiguous categorization of all offense histories. The Offense Class--

Level of Aggressiveness Scale is shown in Table 2.4. For purposes of analysis the youth population has been divided into nonaggressive and aggressive groups. Offense classes 1-3 are primarily nonaggressive in nature, while offense classes 4-6 characterize the most severe offenses involving aggressive acts against persons.

TABLE 2.4

OFFENSE CLASS--LEVEL OF AGGRESSIVENESS SCALE

Offense Class	Type of Offense	Examples
Nonaggressive		
01	One nonserious offense	Substance abuse
02	Offense against self	Drugs, truancy, incorrigibility
03	Offense against property, not harmful to others	Shoplifting, joy riding
Aggressive		
04	Offense against a person indirectly	Car theft, burglary
05	Offense against a person directly, but not physically harmful	Unarmed robbery, purse snatching
06	Offense against a person directly with actual or intended harm	Armed robbery, muggings, assaults, rapes
Unspecified		
07	Unknown	

2.5   Costs

The determination of appropriate allocation of program resources depends on more then the effectiveness of the various program alternatives. It is also essential to weigh these alternatives with an eye toward costs. While cost may sometimes be a secondary consideration in the allocation of resources for human services, relative cost analysis can be a useful tool in focusing attention on a program's strengths and weaknesses. An effort was made to determine both "relative effectiveness" and "relative cost-effectiveness" to aid in the analysis of program success and to support efficient and effective placement decisions. For the purposes of our analysis of relative cost-effectiveness we have limited our cost information to simple aggregate costs as computed on a per diem basis for each of the various services that form the service package for each client.

The computed costs are average costs, and in most cases presume full utilization rates. Where information was incomplete or contradictory, we have assigned rates which represented the lower of competing figures.

In each case, costs per diem are disaggregated from the total cost for any service or facility; no effort has been made to assign incremental costs for special services to a youth. Similarly we have opted to avoid the issues of marginal costs, economies of scale, and utilization rates. The per diem cost per youth, then, is an estimate based upon aggregate reporting of costs for each facility under investigation. To this cost we have added a special surcharge for caseworker cost. Table 2.5.1 summarizes the cost figures utilized in the current study. Table 2.5.2 summarizes the distribution of youth by costs.

2.6 RCEM Analysis[2]

The Relative Cost-Effectiveness Model (RCEM) is a computer-based, mathematical model which has been successfully applied to numerous public programs (social, law enforcement, etc.) for evaluation of client-based social services. The model was originally developed in 1969 to support an evaluation of the Job Corps' cost-effectiveness and has since been refined and expanded so as to apply generally to the evaluation of client-based social services.

In the application to social services, the model analyzes the experience of clients and ranks client groups, e.g., aggressive youth

---

[2]Narrative in this section draws heavily on RCEM description prepared for an earlier study.

TABLE 2.5.1

COSTS PER YOUTH IN VARIOUS PLACEMENTS
FISCAL YEAR 1973-74[a]

Facility	Facility Per Diem Costs	Case worker Surcharge	Total Per Diem Costs	Total Costs	
				3 Months	6 Months
Training School	$44.20	-	$44.20	$3,978	$7,956
Camps	31.63	-	31.63	2,847	5,694
Halfway House	30.22[b]	-	30.22	2,720	5,440
Private Institutions	24.14	-	24.14	2,173	4,346
Adult Correctional Facility[c]	17.54	-	17.54	1,579	3,158
Group Home	13.94[b]	-	13.94	1,255	2,510
Independent Living	6.22[b]	$.86	7.08	637	1,274
Foster Home	5.56[b]	.86	6.72	605	1,210
Relative's Home	3.99[b]	.86	4.85	436	872
Own Home	1.77[b]	.86	2.63	237	474

[a]Source: Based on budget and cost information furnished by the Office of Children and Youth Services, Michigan Department of Social Services.

[b]Educational costs are added to per diem costs based on participation in public school or attention center programs.

[c]Per diem costs are based on a weighted average of males and females at Detroit House of Correction.

vs. nonaggressive youth, according to the effectiveness and cost-effectiveness of services delivered. With respect to the present study, the impact of the services delivered by alternative placements to various client subsets has been defined according to client outcomes and stated in terms of relative outcomes and costs.

TABLE 2.5.2

FREQUENCY DISTRIBUTION OF YOUTH BY COSTS

Per Quarter Costs Per Youth	Frequency	Percent
$ 0 - 499	34	8.2
500 - 999	10	2.4
1,000 - 1,499	43	10.3
1,500 - 1,999	4	1.0
2,000 - 2,499	108	26.0
2,500 - 2,999	33	7.9
3,000 - 3,899	8	1.9
3,900 - 3,978	176	42.3
TOTAL	416	100.0

2.6.1   Outcome Categories

The results of the RCEM itself to a large degree are dependent upon the proper definition of outcomes and the frequency data supporting the existence of those outcomes. (The method utilized to define outcomes is discussed above.)

Once the appropriate outcome category is identified for each client under consideration, the RCEM totals the number of clients assigned to the different categories, thus forming a frequency distribution across the outcome categories. The RCEM can compute the frequency distribution across outcome categories and other client grouping or sub-grouping. Thus, a typical frequency distribution computed by the RCEM would be the number of "young clients" from large urban areas who were assigned to Category 1, to Category 2, and so on.

A client's outcome may be expressed in various ways. For example, a delinquent child who was discharged from state care might be considered as having had successful or unsuccessful treatment. But if outcome categories as unrefined as these are used to formally establish each client's outcome, only relatively unrefined results are feasible through program analysis by any analytic method, including the RCEM. A better way of defining these outcome categories might be "client working or going to school" or "client remanded to criminal court." This type of categorization provides the kind of refinement generally thought to be necessary for the analysis of a social service program.

Examples of the outcome categories ultimately defined for analysis of the Decentralization Project for use with the RCEM have been listed and discussed earlier. (See Combined Outcome Scale.)

2.6.2   Unit Cost

The second attribute of a client's experience is cost. For purposes of analysis, the total cost of operations for each placement under consideration is allocated in appropriate proportion to the various clients sampled by the placement, taking into account the extent to which each client used the resources of the program.

2.6.3   Effectiveness

The third and final attribute of a client's experience is effectiveness, that is, the effectiveness of the services rendered. Associated with the outcome scale is an effectiveness measure which reflects for each client in that category the effectiveness of the services rendered to him. (For some categories this effectiveness is taken to be zero.)

The purpose of the RCEM is to compare various client groups within a social service delivery system. If two such units have clients with similar characteristics and one unit achieves proportionally more outcomes with which greater effectiveness is associated, then it can certainly be concluded that this unit is more effective than the other unit.

2.6.4   RCEM Output

The RCEM, then, accepts computer input data (outcomes, costs, effectiveness), among client groups or units, analyzes the combinations, and produces a quartet of numbers for each pair of client groups or service units:

a.   The average relative effectiveness of the service to the one group as compared with the other.

b.   The probability that one is more or less effective than the other.

c.   The average relative cost-effectiveness of the service to the one group as compared with the other.

d.   The probability that one is more cost-effective than the other.

Relative effectiveness and cost-effectiveness will be fully discussed in Chapter 5. An analysis of the functioning of the Wayne County juvenile justice system follows.

CHAPTER 3
SYSTEM DYNAMICS

3.1   Demographic Profile

The analysis of the dynamics of the Wayne County juvenile justice system has, as its basis, a demographic profile of the Wayne County delinquent state ward population. A detailed demographic profile of the individuals being served by the juvenile justice system in Wayne County is presented in Appendix B. It is sufficient here to summarize those data. First, the delinquent ward population is primarily black and male. Among the male population, blacks are more likely to have committed aggressive offenses than whites. Among females, race is not a factor; females commit almost entirely nonaggressive offenses. See Figure 3.1. Second, males commit their first recorded offense earlier than females. Third, the younger the age at first offense, the greater the probability of subsequent aggressive offenses. Fourth, the older the youth when admitted to state wardship, the more likely the youth has committed an aggressive offense. Fifth, more aggressive youth experience longer periods of delay between first offense and admission to state wardship. Finally, blacks and males experience longer delay periods than whites and females. This demographic survey, as we shall see, has a significant bearing on how youth are processed after adjudication through intake and into their initial placement.

3.2   The Intake and Placement Process: An Overview

The intake process is designed to evaluate the needs of adjudicated youth and subsequently secure a placement that offers treatment commensurate with these needs. The concept is called planned differential placement and is the goal of the intake process. During the 1973-74 fiscal year, planned differential placement was realized through three distinct intake procedures. The first procedure was provided by the Wayne County Juvenile Court staff, who place youth before they are adjudicated to state wardship. The Wayne County Court placed approximately 11 percent of the delinquent state ward population. In the

17

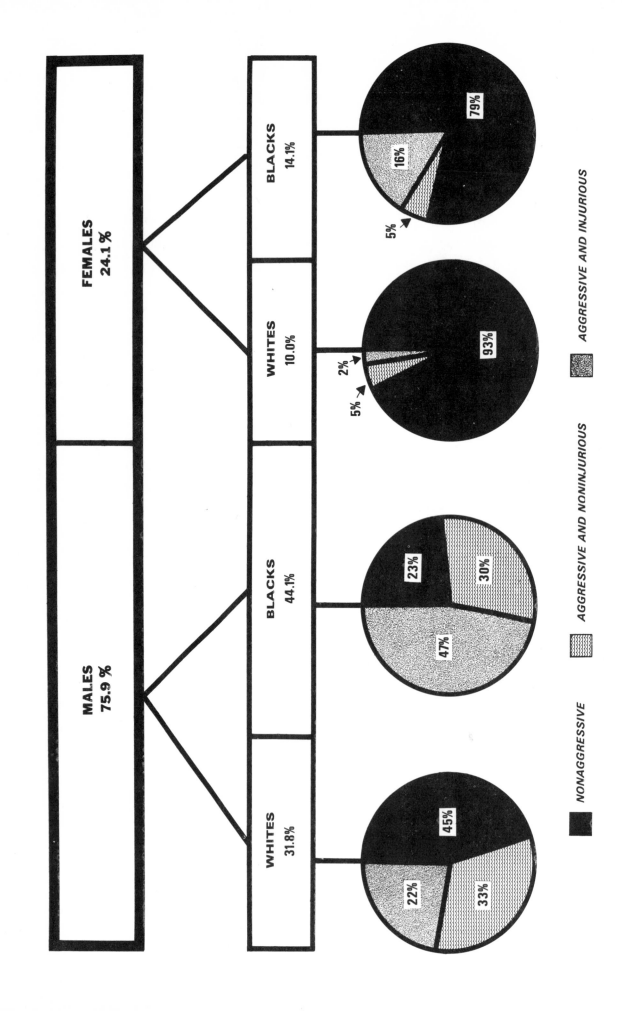

THE DEMOGRAPHIC PROFILE: SEX BY RACE AND LEVEL OF AGGRESSIVENESS

FIGURE 3.1

18

MALES 75.9%

FEMALES 24.1%

WHITES 31.8%

BLACKS 44.1%

WHITES 10.0%

BLACKS 14.1%

45%

22%

33%

47%

30%

23%

93%

2%

5%

79%

16%

5%

NONAGGRESSIVE

AGGRESSIVE AND NONINJURIOUS

AGGRESSIVE AND INJURIOUS

discussion below, these wards will be referred to as "court placed" youth.

The second intake procedure was provided by the Department of Social Services intake staff who make direct placements of wards shortly after their dispositional hearing. Youth are placed either out of their own home or the Wayne County Youth Home. This group of wards comprises 57 percent of the total delinquent population, and will be referred to as "direct placement" youth.

The third intake procedure is furnished by the intake centers. The centers are designed primarily to provide indepth evaluation of new wards in order to better match youth needs with appropriate placement-treatment modalities. The centers are also used for short-term, interim placements while awaiting vacancies in "optimal" facilities. In this case, youth are held until an appropriate facility can be secured. "Intake youth",as these will be called, comprise 32 percent of the delinquent population.

Two intake centers, one male and one female, were operational during the fiscal year. The male intake center on Townsend Street served 136 youth with an average length of stay of 34.5 days, at a cost of $65.26[1] per youth per day. The center's average daily population was 12.8 youth which is equivalent to a utilization rate of 80.3 percent.

The female intake center, at Defer Place, served 54 youth with an average length of stay of 38.1 days at an average daily cost of $13.81 per youth, per day. The average daily population was 5.8 youth and resulted in a utilization rate of 72.7 percent. See Table 3.1 for additional intake center statistics.

---

[1]This per diem is the midpoint between a maximum estimate of $75.55 which includes 75 percent of the salaries paid to intake staff who are not always at the centers, and a minimum estimate of $54.96 which excludes all salaries paid to intake staff who are not always at the centers.

TABLE 3.1

INTAKE CENTER OPERATIONS
Fiscal Year 1973-74

Intake Center	Ca-pac-ity	Number of Youth Served	Days of Care	Ave. Length of Stay (days)	Ave. Daily Popu-lation	Utili-zation Rate	Truancy Rate	Per Diem Costs
Townsend (Male)	16	136	4,687	34.5	12.8	80.3%	41.9%	$65.26
Defer (Female)	8	54	1,628	38.6	5.8	72.7%	49.0%	13.92

3.3 Client Characteristics and Placements of Intake Subpopulations

As stated above, the goal of the intake process is to achieve the planned differential placement of youth relative to their individual needs. The purpose of this section is to determine whether or not the intake process is attaining its goal of planned differential placement. To do this, a two-fold analysis will be employed. First, client characteristics will be examined within each intake procedure to discern whether or not that process is differentially placing its youth according to select characteristics. Second, the three processes will be examined as a system to determine if differential placement exists between as well as within intake processes. See Figures 3.3.1 and 3.3.2.[2]

3.3.1 Court Placed Youth

In general, the Wayne County Court selects nonaggressive, white youth for placement. Specifically, white youth comprise 77.3, and non-aggressive youth 72.7 percent of this subpopulation. This is in sharp

---

[2]To simplify this narrative, only the most significant facts have been included. For a detailed analysis of each demographic characteristic and its interaction with the intake and placement processes, refer to the narrative and tabular presentation of Appendix C.

contrast to the total population characteristics where white youth comprise 42, and nonaggressive youth comprise 45 percent of the total population.

The court institutionalizes almost all of these youth; 93 percent of this subpopulation were placed in institutions. This is significantly above the average 72 percent rate of institutionalization for the total population. Significantly, 89 percent of these youth are placed in private institutions, a rate 3.6 times greater than the population as a whole. Finally, the only youth not institutionalized were one black and two white nonaggressive females, who were placed in community residential care facilities.

3.3.2   Directly Placed Youth

The demographic composition of this subpopulation reflects, with small variation, the composition of the total sample. In essence, directly placed youth are predominantly male and black, and commit a greater proportion of aggressive offenses than nonaggressive offenses.

Directly placed youth are institutionalized 81 percent of the time, while only 14 percent of these youth are placed in community residential care facilities and the remaining five percent in community nonresidential facilities. Directly placed youth in private institutions comprise 20 percent of the total subpopulation and 26 percent of all institutionalized, directly placed youth.

Differential placement does exist within the directly placed subpopulation. Males are institutionalized at a rate of 16 percentage points greater than females, whereas females are placed in community residential care facilities at a rate that is also 16 percentage points greater than males. Moreover, black youth are institutionalized at a rate that is 10 percentage points greater than whites, while whites receive a greater rate of community residential care placements. Finally, nonaggressive youth are placed in institutions at a somewhat lower rate than aggressive youth. In sum, for directly placed youth, males, blacks and aggressive youth have a greater probability of being placed in

22

THE INTAKE PROCESS AND DISTRIBUTION OF PLACEMENTS BY TYPE OF INTAKE PROCEDURE

FIGURE 3.3.1

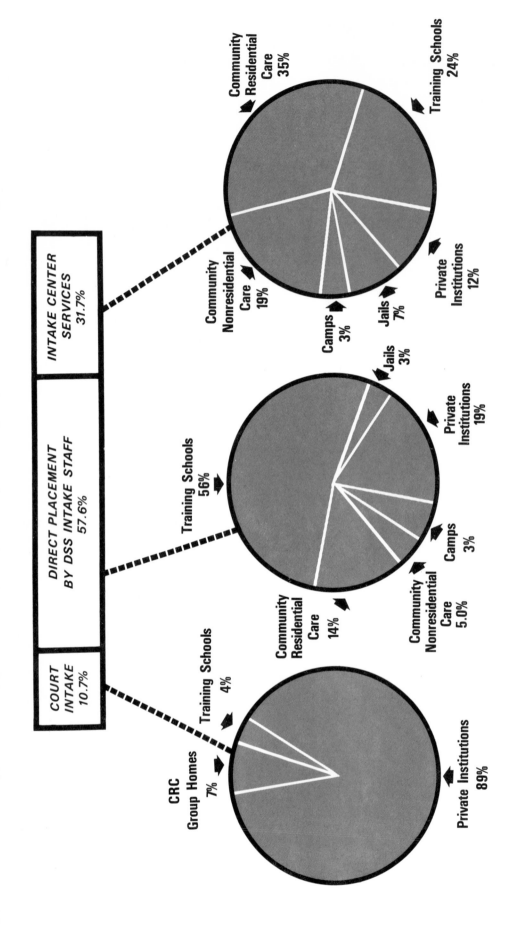

| COURT INTAKE 10.7% | DIRECT PLACEMENT BY DSS INTAKE STAFF 57.6% | INTAKE CENTER SERVICES 31.7% |

COURT

Private Institutions 89%
CRC Group Homes 7%
Training Schools 4%

DIRECT PLACEMENT

Training Schools 56%
Community Residential Care 14%
Community Nonresidential Care 5.0%
Camps 3%
Private Institutions 19%
Jails 3%

INTAKE CENTER

Community Residential Care 35%
Training Schools 24%
Community Nonresidential Care 19%
Camps 3%
Jails 7%
Private Institutions 12%

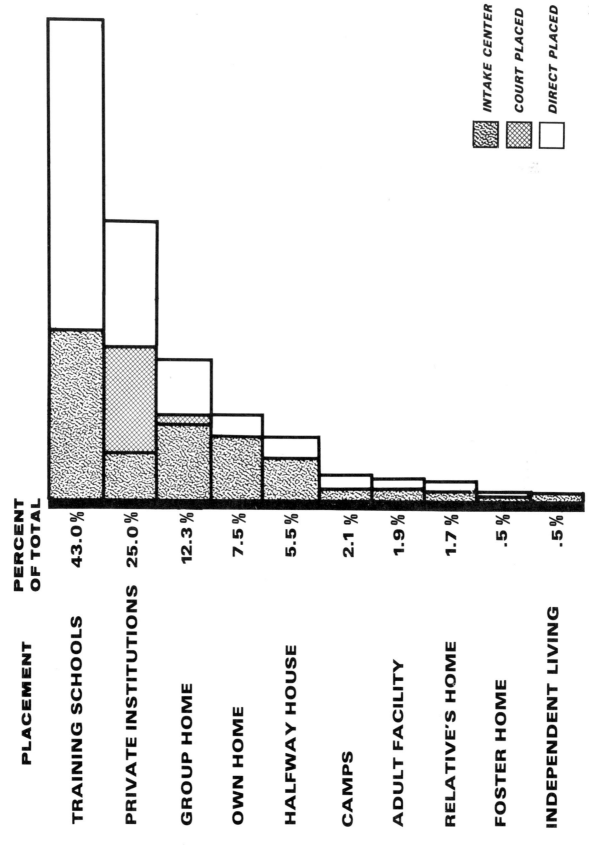

FIGURE 3.3.2

INITIAL PLACEMENT AND INTAKE PROCEDURE
(ROW PERCENTAGES TOTAL 100%)

INTAKE CENTER
COURT PLACED
DIRECT PLACED

PLACEMENT	PERCENT OF TOTAL
TRAINING SCHOOLS	43.0 %
PRIVATE INSTITUTIONS	25.0 %
GROUP HOME	12.3 %
OWN HOME	7.5 %
HALFWAY HOUSE	5.5 %
CAMPS	2.1 %
ADULT FACILITY	1.9 %
RELATIVE'S HOME	1.7 %
FOSTER HOME	.5 %
INDEPENDENT LIVING	.5 %

23

institutions than do females, whites and nonaggressive youth.

3.3.3   Intake Center Placed Youth

The Intake Center subpopulation represents a type of youth that is substantially different from the total population of delinquent youth. There are a greater proportion of males, blacks and aggressive and non-injurious youth in the intake subpopulation than in the total population. Specifically, 84 percent of the intake center placed youth are males, compared to 76 percent of the total population; 65 percent of the intake subpopulation is black, compared to 58 percent of the total population; and 36 percent of the intake population is aggressive and non-injurious, compared to only 25 percent in the total population. Finally, relative to the total population, the intake subpopulation is comprised of proportionately fewer nonaggressive youth and an equivalent proportion of aggressive and injurious youth.

The intake center placements reflect a trend away from the institutionalization that is present in the total population. Only 47 percent of the intake subpopulation was institutionalized, while 19 percent were placed in community nonresidential facilities and 35 percent in community residential care facilities. By contrast, 72 percent of the total population was institutionalized, whereas 10 percent were placed in community nonresidential facilities and 17 percent in community residential care facilities.

Differential placement does result from Intake Center procedures. First, females are placed in institutions and community residential care facilities at a greater rate than males, whereas males are placed in community nonresidential placements at a greater rate than females. Second, whites receive a greater frequency of community residential care placements than do blacks. Finally, aggressive-and-non-injurious youth are institutionalized at a frequency about 19 percentage points greater than the frequency for nonaggressive and aggressive-and-injurious youth. On the other hand, nonaggressive and aggressive-and-injurious youth receive a much greater proportion of community residential care placements than do aggressive-and-noninjurious youth. In sum, for Intake Center placed youth, females and aggressive-and-noninjurious youth have the greatest probability of being institutionalized, while males, blacks, nonaggressive and aggressive-and-injurious youth have the greatest probability of community placement.

3.3.4 The Intake Process Viewed as a Total System

The three intake processes, functioning as a whole, are a precursor to planned differential placement, and represent increasingly complex levels of client evaluation and services. Specifically, the Wayne County Court is placing predominantly white, male, nonaggressive youth in private institutions. These youth are probably the "easiest-to-place" youth from the total population. Directly placed youth reflect the composition of the general population and are the second easiest-to-place group. The offenses committed by this group are much more aggressive than the Wayne County Court group, and receive more public institutional placements. Finally, Intake Center placed youth have filtered through the court and direct placement processes and have been referred to the Intake Center. As a result, these youth represent the most difficult-to-place youth. Significantly, 65 percent of the population have committed aggressive offenses, while only 47 percent are institutionalized. Therefore, the intake centers, while working with the most difficult-to-place subpopulation, are diverting youth away from institutions at a much greater frequency than the other two intake processes.

3.4 Client Characteristics and Initial Placement

The goal of examining initial placement is to determine if there are any differences across placement type in the demographic characteristics and in the personality and attitudinal characteristics of the youth, aside from the intake process through which youth were channeled. Presented below is an overview of only the significant findings associated with the demographic characteristics and attitudinal measures.

3.4.1 Sex and Initial Placement

Males are placed at greater than expected frequencies in institutional and community nonresidential care placements, whereas they are placed at less than expected frequency in community residential care facilities. Conversely, females are placed at greater than expected frequencies in community residential care placements, while they are placed at less than expected frequencies in institutions and community nonresidential care facilities.

3.4.2 Race and Initial Placement

White youth are institutionalized at greater frequencies than black youth, although white youth are placed in private institutions and camps at much greater frequencies than black youth. Black youth are primarily placed in the state training schools. However, black youth receive more community residential care placements than white youth, ostensibly a function of the high representation of blacks in the Intake Center population and their subsequent placements in the community.

3.4.3 Level of Aggressiveness and Initial Placement

Although various intake processes are succeeding in placing youth differentially, the system overall fails to adequately differentiate on the basis of a youth's level of aggressiveness. Approximately 70 percent of all youth are placed in institutions; 74 percent of all aggressive youth are being placed in institutions while 64 percent of all nonaggressive youth (most of whom are status offenders,) are being placed in institutions. The failure to divert nonaggressive state wards from institutions rests with the Wayne County Court which placed all but a few youth in institutions.

3.4.4 Psychological Attributes and Initial Placement

To determine if there are any psychological differences across initial placement, an investigation has been undertaken to measure and evaluate personality and attitudinal characteristics of state wards across placement types. The investigation utilizes a questionnaire to measure the attitudes and opinions of the wards at the beginning and

TABLE 3.4.4

YOUTH OPINION POLL SCORES
(Average Pretest Scores)

SCALE	Maxey BTS				Green Oaks Center (N=20)	Adrian TS		Camps		Community Residential Care	
	Campus Center A (N=50)	Campus Center B (N=73)	Campus Center C (N=50)	Intensive Treatment Program* (N=8)		Males* (N=8)	Females* (N=8)	Nokomis (N=32)	Shawano (N=21)	Males (N=34)	Females (N=18)
Self Esteem	31.9	31.8	32.9	30.0	29.7	34.1	32.5	29.1	26.9	29.0	27.3
Locus of Responsibility	14.0	13.5	13.2	14.1	14.2	14.4	12.6	13.0	13.8	14.1	13.5
Nurturance	13.9	13.2	12.9	12.6	14.2	15.0	14.6	13.5	13.1	11.9	15.5
Social Desirability	13.9	13.6	13.4	14.0	12.8	14.3	14.3	12.1	11.9	12.4	12.0
Psychopathic Delinquency	8.8	9.8	11.5	7.8	8.5	8.3	8.5	10.0	9.5	8.6	8.4
Neurotic Delinquency	13.0	13.5	13.8	12.4	15.7	13.8	12.3	14.7	17.2	13.9	15.9
Subcultural Delinquency	17.3	17.3	17.1	16.6	17.1	18.8	14.3	16.5	18.3	14.9	14.9
Delinquency Total	39.1	40.7	42.5	36.8	41.3	40.8	35.0	41.2	44.7	38.4	38.9
Critical Indicators of PPC	65.2	63.4	60.7	66.5	61.9	68.8	65.1	61.8	60.3	62.4	63.9

*Due to the small sample size these results are not to be compared to other centers or used as a true indication of program effectiveness.

termination of each placement. This methodology permits an evaluation of youth type relative to type of placement, and also reflects the degree of personality and attitudinal change while in this placement. The questionnaire used for this evaluation is the Youth Opinion Poll (YOP) and is described in Appendix C-4.

Table 3.4.4 compares YOP pre-test scores for **both** Wayne County and outstate youth in state operated programs. While we must emphasize that this analysis is preliminary, due to low sample sizes for some groups, there appears to be evidence that placement is indeed controlled to some extent by the "youth type", even though the attitude and typology measures are not part of the placement process.

The scores indicate differences not only between community placements and selected institutional placements, but also illustrate the differences between institutional and the quasi-institutional camp placements. Contrary to our expectations, community youth in comparison to institutional youth generally have:

    (1)   equivalent or lower pre-test scores on the self-esteem scale; and

    (2)   equivalent or lower pre-test scores among the males on the nurturance scale.

In addition, although the sample size is small, there are indications that:

    (3)   community placed youth are likely to score higher than institutional youth on the indicator of neurotic delinquency, exceeded only by the youth placed in Camp Shawono and the highly structured Green Oak Center.

    (4)   community youth achieve scores similar to institutional youth on psychopathic delinquency; and

    (5)   community placed youth achieve lower scores on subcultural delinquency. This finding indicates that community youth may be less socialized to subcultural norms.

These preliminary findings, if substantiated with evidence from a larger sample size, may lay to rest the contention that institutionally placed youth are measurably more "delinquent" than their community placed counterparts. As the study continues, we hope to verify these findings and ascertain the extent to which these measures may be useful as a pre-placement diagnostic tool.

3.5   Summary

The processes of differential intake and differential placement have resulted in the diversion of state wards from institutions.

In the main, this diversion is the result of Intake Center placements; court and direct placed youth continue to be primarily institutionalized. Moreover, because the Intake Center has affected only one-third of the youth, the impact of planned differential placement on institutional diversion has not been as extensive as it might have been. Nonetheless, the entire intake process has facilitated differential placement; indeed, differential placement is a function of a differential intake which then selectively places youth into the programs that are most likely to accept them. Of particular interest is the phenomenon within the Wayne County Court, whereby the easiest-to-place youth are expeditiously placed into private institutions and group homes. Race appears to be a factor in the court placements: white youth are placed by the court at much greater frequencies than black youth and receive a disproportionate percentage of the private institutional placements. Clearly, the court is selectively diverting youth from the state training schools into private institutions. This intake process may work in favor of the black and aggressive youth whose eventual disposition after a lengthy Intake Center stay is most likely to result in community placements. As we shall see, these community placements tend to be the more effective (as well as the more cost-effective) placements.

Preliminary evidence from the Youth Opinion Poll indicates that differential placement of a more subtle nature may be occurring. Although every precaution has been taken to assure uniform practices in the administration of the test, the small sample size and the variations in the physical location of the testing centers require that these preliminary indications of differences be viewed with caution. Despite these caveats, the evidence to date suggests that the Youth Opinion Poll may become increasingly effective for (1) determining the nature of differential placement, and (2) developing a pre-placement diagnostic tool to facilitate more appropriate, effective, and cost-effective placements.

Thus, given the available evidence, it is clear that differential placement is taking place. It is, in part, a tacit decision process; youth are being selected at each decision point in the system and differentially placed by a selective intake process. The most successful differential placements are being effected by the Intake Center, whose difficult-to-place youth are receiving the greatest proportion of institutional diversion and the most varied and specialized placements in the community. In the two chapters that follow, the positive efficacy of both institutional and community programs will be examined.

CHAPTER 4
GOAL ATTAINMENT

The following analysis concerns the community residential care, attention center, and institutional components of the Decentralization Project. In the previous chapter we discussed the dynamics of the intake and placement process. In this section we examine the nature of the principle placement alternatives and the extent to which each of these components reached the service goals established for them.

The community residential care analysis examines the Wayne County facilities and compares their utilization and goal attainment to outstate facilities. The analysis will demonstrate the relative success or failure of the Wayne County facilities with respect to the statewide community residential care system.

The attention center analysis will examine the nature of the attention centers, the differences among the attention center populations, and the relative success of each center in meeting its rehabilitative goals. The impact of the centers on state wards and on the community-at-large will be assessed.

Finally, the institutional components of the Decentralization Project -- specifically, the special diagnostic, intensive treatment, and crisis units--are described, goals are stated, and degree of goal attainment is assessed.

4.1   Community Residential Care

Of all youth served by the Decentralization Project, 17.8 percent were placed in community residential care facilities, primarily in the six Wayne County facilities. Roughly thirty percent of the community residential care placements received halfway house services. The remainder were placed in small group home facilities. Of the females placed through the Wayne County intake process, 21 percent utilized the Defer Place, which serves as a short-term shelter home, but has characteristics that are similar to a group home or halfway house facility. In the discussion that follows each type of facility is described. Next, the Wayne County community residential facilities, components of the Decentralization Project, are compared to the outstate homes on the community residential care goal attainment measures.

4.1.1   Description of Community Residential Care Facilities

Group Homes

The group home is designed for relatively long-term care under the direction of houseparents. The average duration of stay in the group homes is from six to ten months, although this does not indicate a minimum or maximum. An individualized treatment plan is developed for each youth by the group home caseworker, whose goal is to place the youth in a permanent community placement when appropriate behavior goals are reached. Wayne County has four group homes, or 17 percent of the 23 state group home facilities.

Halfway House

The halfway house has the same purpose as the group home, but is structured differently. Unlike the group and shelter homes, which are owned by the houseparents, the halfway house is either owned or leased by the sponsoring agency. Instead of houseparents the home is supervised by workers in eight-hour shifts. The director is on duty at least eight hours, and is "on call" the remainder of the day. Wayne County has two halfway houses, or 17 percent of the 12 halfway houses in the state.

Shelter Homes

The shelter home program involves two types of homes. Both types are under the direction of houseparents. One type is designed to provide short-term care, with a maximum stay of three weeks. Youth may be placed in this type of shelter home for a variety of reasons: a youth needing evaluation for a permanent placement, a youth awaiting a court appearance, or a runaway youth apprehended by the police with no place to go.

The second type is an interim home, where the term of stay per ward may be lengthened to a period of three months. The same type of youth mentioned above may be placed in this home as well as newly adjudicated state wards. In this setting the youth are subjected to intake procedures and in-house treatment before receiving their permanent placement. In Wayne County, there is one home which serves as a shelter home - Defer House. In reality, Defer House is a special combination of the community residential care types and will be considered separately.

4.1.2 Objectives and Measures of Community Residential Care

The primary goal of community residential care is to provide effective residential programs for delinquent youth who require a living environment with more structure than is available through their own families or independent living, but with less structure than that presumed to exist in state institutions. This applies to all three groups of youth served by the project: (1) those placed in a group home who otherwise would be placed in an institution, (2) those placed in a halfway house after institutionalization, and (3) those placed in a shelter home instead of a detention center or jail on an emergency basis pending further evaluation.

However, this broadly stated goal is not sufficient for evaluation purposes. The question remains as to which objectives best describe the term effective community residential care. The objectives and measures of effectiveness can be summarized as follows:

1. To maintain the youth in the home for treatment or evaluation as measured by the number and percentage of youth who truanted.
2. To control delinquent behavior as measured by the number and percentage of youth who had police contacts and/or arrests for reasons other than truancy.
3. To attain educational and vocational skills as measured by the number and percentage of youth who participated successfully in an educational, vocational,

and/or employment program.

4. To prepare youth for subsequent placement as measured by
   the number, percentage, and module of youth who were released successfully; and by the nature of the next placement.

These objectives and measures serve as the basis for the discussion
below.

Utilization

Table 4.1.2 illustrates that Wayne County Community Residential
Care facilities compare favorably with outstate facilities. Specifically, Wayne County group homes utilization rates are higher than those
of the rest of the state, although their halfway houses, at 60.7 percent utilization, are about eight percentage points lower than the
statewide average.

Truancy

On truancy measures, Wayne County group homes were considerably
below the state average at five percent, compared to 27.9 percent for
the state average, Wayne County excluded. Wayne County halfway houses,
on the other hand, have truancy rates higher than the rest of the
state.

Recidivism

On the recidivism measures(police contacts and arrests)Wayne
County group homes are less successful in reducing crime than outstate
homes, while for halfway houses recidivism measures are not significantly
different.

Skill Attainment

Both Wayne County and outstate group homes and halfway houses
have demonstrated considerable success in enlisting participation in
school or work programs. The group home figures, which are drawn from
a larger sample and are more reliable, demonstrate a considerably higher
participation and success rate for Wayne County group homes. The

TABLE 4.1.2

COMPARISON OF WAYNE COUNTY COMMUNITY RESIDENTIAL CARE FACILITIES WITH OUTSTATE FACILITIES

Facility	Capacity	Utilization Rate	Truancy Rate[a]	Recidivism and Goal Attainment (in percentages)						
				Police contacts and arrests	Skill Programs			Release Status		
					Satis-factory	Unsatis-factory	Did not participate	Satis-factory	Unsatis-factory	
Group Homes[b]										
Outstate	134	82.6	27.9	5	73	6	21	58	42	
Wayne County	16	86.6	5.0	15	92	8	0	33	67	
Halfway Houses[c]										
Outstate	141	69.6	15.0	5	81	7	12	60	40	
Wayne County	24	60.7	24.0	6	74	12	14	50	50	
Defer House	8	72.7	44.0	0	63	13	24	25	75	

[a]Percent of all youth who truanted at least once.

[b]Based on FY 1973-74 data, goal attainment measures.

[c]Based on third quarter of 1974 goal attainment measures.

accessability of the attention centers in Wayne County is clearly an effective adjunct to Wayne County group homes.

Release Status

The least encouraging data in the comparative study relates to release status. Wayne County group homes, and to a lesser extent the halfway houses, are achieving fewer satisfactory releases. This situation may well be aggravated by the unsupportive character of the homes' location, and may reflect the more global problem of rehabilitation in a high crime urban environment.

Defer House

Table 4.1.2 clearly indicates that Defer House compares unfavorably on all measures of goal attainment. The short-term nature of the program and the transient nature of the pre-placement population do not allow realistic comparison of Defer with other programs.

4.2   Attention Center Services

The attention center programs were designed initially to be adjuncts to the intake centers in Wayne County and were to provide nonresidential, remedial programming in education, employment, job placement, individual and group counseling and substitute parental care. In the third year of the project, FY 1973-74, a third functionally similar attention center opened in Benton Harbor, but has since ceased operation. A fourth center in Muskegon began operation in November 1974 and has community outreach and delinquency prevention as its main operational goals. What follows are evaluations of individual centers.

4.2.1   The Wayne County Attention Centers

Wayne County has two functionally similar attention centers, one on the east side, the other on the west side of Detroit. Both centers are nonresidential and designed to serve two types of youth populations. The first type of youth are delinquent state wards placed in the community or Intake Center; the second type of youth are nonadjudicated youth from the community that immediately surrounds the attention centers.

For the adjudicated youth, the centers provide educational,
vocational, recreational and counseling services on a rigorously disci-
plined, daily schedule. Emphasis is upon delinquency treatment. At
least minimal service was made available to 201 community placed youth
and 122 male and 27 female youth who were placed at the Townsend Street
and Defer House Intake Centers.

For the nonadjudicated youth, the centers provide low structure
programs, which are for the most part recreational. These youth are not
required to participate on a regularly scheduled basis; their involvement is voluntary. Emphasis here is upon delinquency prevention.

There were some basic differences in function and structure between the East and Westside Attention Centers during fiscal year
1973-74. First, a major proportion of the Eastside's referrals were
intake youth placed at the Townsend Intake Center or from Defer House.
The Westside serviced no Intake Center youth. Second, the Westside
Center's prevention capabilities were extremely hindered due to their
transitory residence in Don Bosco Hall[1] while awaiting completion of
the new Westside Center's construction. These structural and functional
differences between the centers must be given careful consideration to
accurately determine the effects of treatment relative to the type of
youth served at each center.

The effects of treatment at the attention centers are difficult to ascertain. First, due to large discrepancies in individual
emotional and educational capabilities, program impact must be measured with regard to an individual's relative improvement while partic-
pating at the center. Certainly, the successful completion of the
G.E.D. program for one youth may not be as significant as the

---

[1]Don Bosco Hall is a private insitutional facility located in
the inner city. The facility has a capacity for 52 males, ages 13-16
years, and serves primarily Wayne County youth.

successful completion of the special education program by another, more educationally deprived, youth. Second, this relative individual improvement must also be weighted relative to its increasing social utility. Assuming that these youth are equally motivated towards employment, the youth that completed the G.E.D. has a greater probability of obtaining employment and as a result that completion has greater social utility than the completion of the special education program. Hence, program impact is dependent upon the type of youth served and the social utility of the skills attained while participating at the Centers.

Unfortunately, it is impossible to obtain measures of relative individual improvement because pre- and post-educational and technical skill achievement tests are not consistently administered. However, some indications of program impact can be derived by examining the program goal attainment of attention center participants relative to program goal attainment of nonattention center participants. Further, an indepth analysis of attention center dynamics can add additional information regarding the program impact of attention center services.

4.2.1.1 Attention Center Services Versus Other Services

As can be seen in Table 4.2.1.1 both module 3 and 5 attention center youth attain twice the frequency of positive educational outcomes as do other community placed nonattention center youth. Institutional youth achieve a slightly greater proportion of positive educational outcomes then do attention center youth. Moreover, attention center youth attain more positive employment results for both module 3 and 5 youth, then their nonattention center counterparts in the community and institution. Finally, module 3 attention center youth achieved approximately the same frequency of positive offense outcomes as did other module 3 and module 4 youth. However, module 5 attention center youth attained a slightly larger frequency of negative offense outcomes, indicating a somewhat greater recidivism rate than for other youth.

This goal attainment analysis does give a crude indication of how various programs are doing. However, some outcomes are merely an artifact of treatment modality and not a true reflection of that modality's total impact. For example, institutionalized youth, by definition, cannot participate in an employment experience until they are released. Similarly, a community placed youth has a greater opportunity to come into contact with the law during his placement than does his institutionalized counterpart. Hence, no real indication of the social utility of the program is obtainable through this analysis. A much more informative analysis can be realized by examining, in a very specific manner, the program dynamics of the Wayne County attention centers.

4.2.1.2 The Westside Attention Center

The Westside Attention Center impact on its youth appears to be less than optimal, primarily because the social utility of the treatment received by a majority of youth at the Center was not commensurate with their needs subsequent to discharge or release from state wardship. It must be stressed, however, that this is not necessarily a problem isolated at the Westside Center, but reflects a weakness of the delinquency treatment system in general. This point will become quite clear below.

During fiscal year 1973-74, 70 percent of the Westside's population were module 5 youth. That is, these youth had been placed at the Center after release from public or private institutional care. The remaining 30 percent were module 3 youth, state adjudicated wards who have only received community placements.[2] Average length of participation for all youth in this program was 3.1 months.

As was seen above, initial review of the Westside's data reveals an immediate positive impact on its youth. Specifically, 9.7 percent of the youth recidivated while participating at the Center. This is comparable to the recidivism rate of all Wayne County module 3 and 5 state wards, who did not participate in an attention center program; their rate of recidivism for the fiscal year was 7.3 percent. Moreover,

---

[2]This analysis excludes 3 module 3 and 8 module 4 youth placed at the center. The module 4 youth were youth who were placed at Don Bosco Hall and also participated in the Attention Center's activities while placed there.

TABLE 4.2.1.1

PROGRAM GOAL ATTAINMENT:
ATTENTION CENTER AND NONATTENTION CENTER PARTICIPANTS

| | Program Goal Attainment | | | | | |
| | Education | | Employment | | Offenses | |
Placement Type and Program Participants	Positive	Negative	Positive	Negative	Positive	Negative
Community Placements (N=341)	38.4	61.6	32.0	68.0	92.4	7.6
Attention Center Participants (N=71)	76.4	23.9	43.5	56.5	89.3	10.7
Westside Center (N=36)	73.7	26.6	42.9	57.1	90.4	9.6
Module 3 (N=13[a])	80.6	19.4	33.5	66.5	93.3	6.7
Module 5 (N=23)	69.7	30.3	48.5	51.5	88.5	11.5
Eastside Center (N=35)	79.0	21.0	44.0	56.0	88.0	12.0
Module 3 (N=7)	72.2	27.8	41.7	58.3	95.6	4.4
Module 5 (N=12)	73.9	26.1	52.2	47.8	83.3	16.7[b]
Intake Center (N=16)	85.7	14.3	39.1	60.9	-	-
NonAttention Center Participants (N=270)	28.2	71.8	28.8	71.2	93.0	7.0
Module 3 (N=123)	31.3	68.7	25.6	74.4	92.5	7.5
Module 5 (N=145)	25.3	74.7	31.2	68.8	92.7	7.3
Institutional Placements						
Module 4 (N=161)	79.6	20.4	2.9	97.1	95.5	4.5

[a] Average number of participants per month.
[b] Only truancy data is reported. Offenses while AWOL are unknown, however 42 percent of the Townsend and 49 Defer populations truanted for at least one day.

74 percent of all the youth were involved in educational programs, 43 percent in employment programs, and 64 percent in recreational programs. This rate of participation for Westside Center youth is 46 percentage points greater in education and 13 percentage points greater in employment than the rate of participation for all Wayne County state wards.[3]

Unfortunately, the program strength demonstrated above is mitigated by the fact that Westside attendants are predominantly module 5 youth who are in preparation for release or about to reach the age of discharge from state wardship. In general, module 5 youth require the acquisition of educational and technical skills that will give them at least a minimum probability of obtaining unsubsidized employment once they are discharged. As Table 4.2.1.2 indicates, only two percent of the youth were involved in outside unsubsidized employment compared to 47 percent who were involved in a subsidized program. Furthermore, only 16 percent of all the youth were in the G.E.D. program, whereas 26 percent were in the pre G.E.D. and 28 percent were in the special education programs. Therefore, the majority of youth participated in programs that provided only very elementary educational and technical skills. As a result, it is unlikely that the module 5 youth are receiving treatment that adequately prepares them for independent functioning once they are released or discharged.

This argument is not intended to imply that the Westside Center is not treating the youth, especially with regard to their individual needs. On the other hand, what it does state is that module 5 youth are participating in programs that are too elementary to effect adequate independent functioning once these youth are released from wardship. Moreover, the average length of stay in program for module 5 youth is 3.0 months and does not, on the whole, allow enough time for staff or youth to progress through more than one educational level or job placement. As a result, the remedial services provided at the Center are

_____

[3]Source: "Decentralization Project: Goal Attainment Report, Year-End Summary, FY 1973-74, October, 1974."

TABLE 4.2.1.2

WAYNE COUNTY ATTENTION CENTER PROGRAM DYNAMICS

Attention Center, Participant Status and Sex	Average Length of Stay in Program (In Months)	Average Number of Participants Per Month	Percentages of Participants in Special Programs[a]							
			Education				Employment			Recreation
			Special Education	Pre G.E.D.	G.E.D. and College Prep	Totals	Sub-sidized	Unsub-sidized	Totals	All Activities
West Side Center:[b] (N=87)	3.0	36.1	30.5	26.6	16.6	73.7	41.6	1.4	43.0	64.5
Module 3 (N=26)	3.9	13.4	34.3	28.4	17.9	80.6	37.8	0.7	33.5	66.4
Males (N=21)	4.5	10.8	40.7	31.5	15.7	87.9	37.0	0.9	37.9	74.1
Females (N=5)	1.6	2.6	7.7	15.4	26.9	50.0	15.4	0.0	15.4	34.6
Module 5 (N=61)	3.0	22.7	28.2	25.6	15.9	69.7	46.7	1.8	48.5	63.4
Males (N=48)	2.0	19.4	30.9	26.3	13.9	71.1	49.5	2.1	51.6	68.6
Females (N=13)	3.0	3.3	12.1	21.2	27.3	60.6	30.3	0.0	30.3	33.3
East Side Center:[c] (N=218)	2.0	43.6	32.3	28.9	19.3	80.5	48.9	0.0	48.9	58.9
Intake Center (N=136)	1.5	16.1	37.9	29.8	18.0	85.7	39.1	0.0	39.1	80.7
Males (N=109)	1.4	12.1	44.6	31.4	15.7	91.7	43.0	0.0	43.0	84.3
Females (N=27)	1.8	4.0	17.5	25.0	25.0	67.5	27.5	0.0	27.5	70.0
Module 3 (N=37)	2.4	7.2	34.7	36.1	1.4	72.2	41.7	0.0	41.7	47.2
Males (N=24)	2.3	4.5	35.6	33.3	2.2	71.1	55.6	0.0	55.6	48.9
Females (N=13)	2.5	2.7	33.3	40.7	0.0	74.0	22.2	0.0	22.2	44.4
Module 5 (N=36)	3.9	11.5	32.2	36.5	5.2	73.9	52.2	0.0	52.2	28.7
Males (N=22)	3.6	6.6	42.4	42.4	0.0	84.8	63.6	0.0	63.6	30.3
Females (N=14)	4.3	4.9	18.4	28.6	12.2	59.2	36.7	0.0	36.7	26.5
Long-term Participants (N=9)	14.7	8.8	33.0	21.6	43.2	97.8	68.2	0.0	48.9	58.9
Males (N=5)	17.3	5.0	40.0	20.0	40.0	100.0	80.0	0.0	80.0	60.0
Females (N=4)	11.4	3.8	23.6	23.6	47.4	94.6	52.6	0.0	52.6	78.9
GRAND TOTALS (N=305)	2.3	79.7	31.5	27.9	18.1	77.5	45.5	0.6	46.1	61.5

[a]These percentages are relative to the Average Number of Participants Per Month.

[b]Data for the West Side Center excludes three module 2 and eight module 4 youth. Length of stay data reflects 12 months of data. The program computations reflects nine months of extant data. Reports for the fourth calendar quarter of 1974 are not available.

[c]Data for the East Side Center are based on nine months of extant data. Reports from the third calendar quarter of 1974 are not available.

[d]These calculations excludes long-term participants.

necessary but not sufficient in meeting the needs of the module 5 clientele. Most assuredly, the responsibility for the great magnitude of module 5 remedial programming must be placed with the placement-treatment modalities that worked with the youth prior to the attention center assignment.

4.2.1.3 The Eastside Attention Center

The Eastside Attention Center's impact upon its youth appears to be generally positive, given that two-thirds of the youth in the program are being prepared for placement in other treatment modalities. Sixty-three percent of the youth served at the Eastside Center are newly adjudicated Intake Center wards,[4] while the remaining 37 percent are community placed module 3 and 5 wards. Total population average length of participation in program was 2.0 months. Significantly, Intake Center youth averaged only 1.5 months, whereas nonintake youth averaged 3.3 months.

Program emphasis is upon remedial education and technical skills. Eighty percent of the youth were involved in either the special or pre G.E.D. education programs. Forty-nine percent of the youth participated in subsidized employment programs. More advanced programs were much less frequently used. Only 20 percent of the youth were in G.E.D. or higher educational programs, and no youth were able to obtain unsubsidized employment.

The positive impact of the remedial programming of the Eastside Center manifests itself in the subsequent placement of Intake Center youth. As will be shown in Chapter 5, for all placement-treatment modalities Intake Center youth respond more effectively and cost-effectively than directly placed or Wayne County Court placed youth. It is impossible to determine the independent effects of the Attention Center

---

[4]This statistic is at variance with published quarterly report data from the Eastside Center itself, which indicates that Intake Center youth compose only 50 percent of their population. However, their statistics include 27 Defer House females listed as nonintake Center participants, which, when included with the remaining Intake Center participants, raises the Intake Center total to 63 percent.

and the intake centers. However, examined together as a short-term, first placement, remedial programming modality, there is strong evidence of greater performance in subsequent treatment modalities.

For module 3 and 5 youth who were not placed at the Intake Center, the Eastside Center exhibited many of the same weaknesses as did the Westside Center. Too few of these youth participated at the more advanced educational levels or in unsubsidized employment. Moreover the three-month average length of participation in the Center's activities simply precluded a level of educational and vocational attainment needed to prepare youth for independent living once he is discharged from wardship. In short, the Eastside Attention Center programming has met individual needs of youth but has not necessarily provided them the tools that will permit a successful adjustment upon release. The programs have been relatively short-term in nature and have largely benefited those youth who are novices in the delinquency treatment system and respond favorably to intensive, remedial programming.

4.2.1.4 Impact on the Community-at-Large

Both attention centers are located in areas of high poverty, crime and delinquency. It is the purpose of this section to determine what, if any, impact the centers have had upon nonwards whose participation at the centers is strictly voluntary. It is impossible to measure this impact directly, however, an informative overview of delinquency in Detroit can be developed, from which limited inferences can be made about attention center impacts.

Table 4.2.1.4 serves as the focus of this discussion. It demonstrates that in areas of Detroit not served by either attention center, total juvenile offenses decreased by 41 percent between 1969 and 1973. During the same period, total juvenile offenses in those areas served by attention centers decreased by 61 percent, a 20-percentage point additional reduction compared to the nonattention center areas. Moreover, Part I juvenile offenses decreased by 57 percent between 1969 and 1973 in the attention areas compared to 33 percent in the nonattention center areas during the same period. Part II

TABLE 4.2.1.4

INCIDENCE OF CRIME AND DELINQUENCY IN DETROIT BY RESIDENCE
IN SELECTED CENSUS TRACTS, 1969-1973

Year[a] and Type of Offense	West Side Attention Center[d]		East Side Attention Center[e]		Both Attention Centers		Areas of Detroit Not Served By Attention Centers[f]	
	Number of Offenses	Percent Change	Number of Offenses	Percent Change	Number of Offenses	Percent Change	Number of Offenses	Percent Change
1969								
Part I Offenses[b]	366	--	472	--	838	--	4,762	--
Part II Offenses[c]	276	--	173	--	449	--	2,473	--
Total Offenses	561	--	645	--	1,287	--	7,236	--
1971								
Part I Offenses	267	-27.0	308	-34.7	572	-31.7	3,840	-19.4
Part II Offenses	178	-35.5	109	-37.0	287	-36.1	1,950	-21.1
Total Offenses	445	-20.1	417	-35.3	862	-33.0	5,790	-20.0
1972								
Part I Offenses	240	-34.9	192	-59.3	432	-48.4	3,020	-36.6
Part II Offenses	87	-68.5	78	-54.9	165	-63.3	1,589	-35.7
Total Offenses	327	-41.7	270	-58.1	597	-53.6	4,609	-36.3
1973								
Part I Offenses	132	-63.9	158	-66.5	360	-57.0	3,172	-33.4
Part II Offenses	46	-83.3	93	-46.2	139	-69.0	1,066	-56.9
Total Offenses	178	-68.3	251	-61.1	429	-66.7	4,238	-41.4

[a] 1970 data was unavailable.

[b] Includes more serious offenses such as homicide, rape, robbery, assaults, burglary, larceny, etc.

[c] Includes the less serious offenses such as weapons offense, disorderly conduct, curfew violation and various types of truancies.

[d] Includes the twenty census tracts immediately surrounding the Westside Attention Center.

[e] Includes the seventeen census tracts immediately surrounding the Eastside Attention Center.

[f] Includes the remainder of Detroit.

juvenile offenses also demonstrated a marked decrease during the 1969-1973 period, with the nonattention center area showing a reduction of 57 percent and the attention center areas a somewhat larger reduction of 69 percent.

Unfortunately, this data cannot be interpreted without a series of qualifications. First, no population controls have been used in evaluating this data. Hence population flow out of Detroit, especially in areas of high crime and poverty, is not known. Second, police and court practices regarding the arrest and adjudication of youth are not adequately known. Petitions to Wayne County Juvenile Court from the Detroit Police Department dropped 19 percent between 1970 and 1973. Third, the fact that Westside Center was providing minimal community outreach during their recent interim residence in Don Bosco Hall further mitigates the cause-effect relation between the attention center prevention services and the delinquency statistics. In sum, there is a strong correlation between the significant reduction in juvenile delinquency within proximal distance of the attention centers. However in no way can this reduction be attributed solely to the attention centers.

4.2.1.5 Summary: Wayne County Attention Centers

In general, the attention centers have been able to provide intensive, short-term, remedial services to Intake Center youth. However, these same services do not meet the educational and vocational needs of youth who are about to be released or discharged from wardship especially when appropriate remedial programming has not been obtained earlier in the delinquency services system.

The attention centers do appear to have some impact upon curbing the incidence of delinquency in areas immediately surrounding the attention centers. The magnitude of this impact is unknown.

4.2.2 The Berrien County Attention Center

The Berrien County Attention Center was developed as a response to the rapid increase in juvenile delinquency in Berrien County in general and Benton Harbor in particular. The Center, unable to adequately meet the needs of the state ward population or develop any recognizable function for the Berrien County community, discontinued operation approximately one year and six months after its inception. The onus for the Center's failure rests primarily on administrative difficulties. However, the Berrien County Juvenile Court policy of diverting youth from the Juvenile Court system almost ensured minimal long-term utilization of the Center as a treatment program for state wards. Once immediate and future Berrien County delinquency needs were accurately assessed, an evolution from the attention center concept to a Multi-Agency Services Center began to develop.

This presentation includes a summary of the reasons for the failure of the Berrien County Attention Center and the reasons behind the evolution towards the Multi-Agency Services Center. The Attention Center's objectives were two-fold: (1) program state wards away from further deviance, and (2) guide the county in its efforts to better cope with delinquency oriented problems. Unfortunately, neither objective was realized.

The staff did develop rudimentary recreational, employment and counseling programs, although the program's efficacy was highly questionable. In the Center's first ten months of operation, from July 1973 to May 1974, 84 state wards were referred for treatment, of which only 47 received "treatment." The recidivism rate for 47 wards who received attention center treatment was 19 percent, while the recidivism rate for those who did not receive treatment was only four percent. This poor statistical reflection on the Center's delinquency treatment function was, in the main, due to poor staff organization and inadequate program development.

On the community development level, there was even less accomplishment. The attitude of the Center's director precluded any real opportunity for local involvement in the Center's activities. The director's philosophy placed community organization at a very low priority; no ongoing community organization activities were initiated.

Even if the Center had achieved its first objective--the reduction of delinquent behavior among state wards--local juvenile court policy resulted in a marked decrease in commitments to court and state wardship. Hence the demand for the Center's services would be much less than in the past.

The policy of the Court has been to divert youth from the formal machinery of the juvenile justice system by strengthening community resources. Two initiatives in particular have reflected the court's efforts to strengthen local resources: (1) the creation of a youth services bureau, and (2) the construction of a new detention facility.

The Berrien County Youth Services and Assistance Bureau began its operation in July 1973. In its first year and a half of activity, the Bureau served 1,523 youth, some of whom might otherwise be adjudicated and eventually made state wards.

The Berrien County Juvenile Detention Center began its operation in April 1974. The Detention Center reflects the Court's policy to keep more difficult-to-handle youth in a secure near-to-home facility thereby reducing the need for programs such as state-operated institutions and other services. As of February 1975, the Detention Center has provided services to 221 youth in detention and 41 youth in its rehabilitation program.

With these relatively new resources available, it should be no surprise that commitments to state wardship have declined 68 percent from 66 in 1971 to 21 in 1974 while the number of juvenile arrests during the same period remained relatively constant. See Table 4.2.2.

After a thorough evaluation of the Attention Center's function, the Office of Children and Youth Services decided to close the Attention Center by the end of December, 1974. During October, 1974, a task force was created to determine if the Attention Center building could be utilized to benefit Berrien County youth.

It was agreed by all members of this task force that the

TABLE 4.2.2

JUVENILE DELINQUENCY INDICATORS:
BERRIEN COUNTY, 1967-1974

Calendar Year	Juvenile Arrests		Commitments to Court Wardship		Commitments to State Wardship		Youth Service Bureau Referrals	
	N	%[a] Change	N	% Change	N	% Change	N	% Change
1967	1,196	-	1,089	-	73	-	-	-
1968	1,187	-0.1	1,185	8.8	65	-10.9	-	-
1969	1,593	33.2	1,321	21.3	77	5.5	-	-
1970	1,649	37.9	1,156	6.1	54	-31.5	-	-
1971	1,901	58.9	1,373	26.1	66	- 9.6	-	-
1972	1,989	66.3	1,293	18.7	41	-43.8	-	-
1973	2,145	79.3	1,096	0.6	24	-67.1	499[b]	-
1974	1,984	65.9	896	-17.6	21	-71.2	1,024	2.6

[a]All percents are relative to the base year, 1967.

[b]For six months of operation.

Center's function, if needed, be made consistent with the predominant focus of the county youth serving agencies: the diversion of youth from the juvenile justice system and the prevention of delinquent behavior. The task force did feel that there was a need for additional diversion oriented services that could be provided in the Center. Importantly, the task force decided not to create another youth serving agency, but to work together and to coordinate their services through the Center, thereby enhancing the effectiveness of their own agencies in diverting youth from the juvenile justice system.

The Inter-Agency Youth Services Network Council has been created through the efforts of this task force. The purpose of this Council is to coordinate service development and delivery in Berrien

County, with a strong emphasis on youth who are from areas with a high incidence of delinquency. A goal of this Council will be to administer a Multi-Agency Service Center which will be housed in the present attention center facility. The new center will hopefully provide a wide range of services to children and parents who reside in Greater Benton Harbor and Burton Township communities.

In concluding the discussion of the Berrien County Attention Center program, it can be said that the initial failure was undoubtedly due to inadequate service delivery and the lack of community coordination and organization. However, given the emphasis of the Berrien County Juvenile Court upon diversion from the court system, it appears that, regardless of the functional capabilities of the Center, its activities would have been directed to an increasingly smaller number of state wards. Hence, the change to the Multi-Agency Service Center should facilitate and improve the general efficacy of the Berrien County youth serving agencies and greatly improve the cost-effectiveness of services for troubled youth.

4.2.3   The Muskegon Attention Center

The Muskegon Attention Center began providing services to youth in October, 1974. As a result, the data sample reflecting program impact is as yet too small to yield meaningful results. It is important to note, however, that the Muskegon Attention Center's function is quite different from the centers in Detroit. Hence the theoretical function of the Muskegon Center will be discussed briefly.

Aside from providing a limited number of counseling and employment opportunities, the Center's emphasis is upon community outreach and development. In fact, of the ten positions slated for youth and family involvement, only two are designed for inhouse counseling duties. The remainder will be interacting with youth in the schools, on the streets, in youth hang-outs, and so on.

In the Center's first quarter of operation, all staff received training in counseling techniques and drug crisis intervention.

Furthermore, emphasis has been placed upon program publicity. This entails making the Center not only known to youth, but to potential referral sources such as police and court personnel, school officials, parents in the target groups and the like. Public speaking, radio and television appearances are also scheduled to increase community awareness of the Center.

The outreach approach has generated 42 referrals to staff counselors, 53 youth have been involved in recreation programs and more than 200 youth have been contacted by youth outreach workers. In addition, the volunteer coordinators have recruited a group of ten volunteers.

In short, the Muskegon Attention Center is in the process of implementing the youth services bureau model of delinquency prevention. The goal of this model is to define the individual and group needs of target area youth through community outreach. Once the needs are defined, local youth and adults will be organized by the Center to hopefully alleviate the stresses and problems of youth that lead to delinquent behavior.

4.3   Institutional Services

Prior to the introduction of the Decentralization Project, nearly all Wayne County delinquent state wards were institutionalized. Because of Decentralization, Wayne County has been able to develop community-based alternatives to cope with delinquent youth. These alternatives have had a noticeable impact on the type of youth being sent to the training schools, and on the scope of services rendered at the Maxey Boys' Training School in particular. Staff have indicated that a smaller number of youth are being referred to the training school but that a larger proportion of youth are "harder" delinquents or have severe personality problems.

The smaller number of youth have enabled the training school to reallocate its resources to meet the needs of these youth in the form of specialized programs. The specialized programs are physically

located in the Reception Center of the Maxey Boys' Training School. The
Reception Center previously devoted most of its space to intake diagnosis
and reevaluation of youth being transferred to other institutional programs. Because of intake services rendered in the community, the Decentralization Project has enabled many youth to be placed directly into
the training school program, requiring only minimal screening in the
Reception Unit. This allowed two wings of the Reception Center to be
allocated to specialized programs. Currently there are three programs
in the Reception Center:the Intake Diagnostic Program, the Intensive
Treatment Program, and the Crisis Intervention and Reassessment Program.
Each are evaluated below in terms of the objectives established for
each program.

4.3.1   The Intake Diagnostic Program

The Intake Diagnostic Program provides initial diagnostic and
assessment services for youth entering the institution from the community. The diagnostic process includes both a psychological assessment
and a physical screening which includes dental and eye checks as well
as a check on overall physical health. The complete diagnostic procedure requires from two to three weeks to complete.

Since March 1973 all counties have been sending youth to
institutions through a direct referral process. A modified screening
is conducted for youth admitted through this direct referral process.
These youth receive the health screening and are interviewed by one
counseling staff member of the Intake Diagnostic Unit. This interview
allows the staff member to gain an impression of the youth which can be
forwarded to the unit the boy is to enter. It also allows the staff
member to provide the youth with information about the training school
facility and program, and to prepare him for entering his assigned
unit. Should this interview reveal serious problems which would seem
to preclude placing the youth directly into the open program the staff
member can place the youth in the Intake Diagnostic Unit for further
evaluation. Such a decision would be made if, for example, the inter-
viewer determined that the youth was in the process of withdrawal from

an addictive drug.

The primary purpose of the Intake Diagnostic Program is to continue providing diagnostic services for those youth whose problems are too serious to permit an immediate placement in a specific treatment unit. The objectives of the program relate to this primary purpose.

Objective 1: To assess wards referred from the community.

In FY 1973-74 the Intake Diagnostic Unit assessed 329 youth. These youth were processed through a three-week cycle of activity which would take them through screening programs to assess physical health, dental health, psychological functioning and educational achievement and ability. The cycle was completed for each youth within 2½ weeks from its start. At that time a placement choice could be made but due to the lack of available space in many programs the actual placement could take a considerably longer time. Some youth remained in the Intake Diagnostic Unit longer than the three-week period waiting for an opening in the desired unit. The actual assessment process, however, was completed within the three-week time.

Objective 2: To initiate appropriate therapeutic programs through such activities as education, individual and group counseling, and recreation.

Although the primary purpose of the unit is diagnostic, every effort is made to involve the youth in appropriate therapeutic activities. As specific needs are identified remedial activities commence. A full-time staff doctor provides an initial diagnostic health screening and a program of medical care is begun. If serious medical problems are found the youth can be referred to the University of Michigan Medical Hospital. A dentist is available on a part-time basis. After the diagnostic screening, dental services are scheduled and may be initiated while the youth is still in the reception unit. An eye examination is provided and glasses are prescribed if necessary.

Certain activities occur on a regularly scheduled basis. Wood shop and arts and crafts are provided each week to each youth at a prescribed time. The gym is available for recreation under the supervision of the recreational director. Group counseling sessions occur each week usually on Monday evening. The psychologist and teacher test each youth during his diagnostic cycle; testing is done each day and youth are tested as their schedule permits. Individual counseling is provided to each youth, although this is not a scheduled activity in the sense that a shop class or a psychological testing program are scheduled events. Psychiatric services are a part of the diagnostic process if they are necessary. Presently, there is no psychiatrist assigned to the unit. The staff can consult other psychiatrists to evaluate youth and arrange transfers to mental hospitals if necessary.

Objective 3: To make appropriate placement decisions.

Each youth is evaluated in terms of his strengths and weaknesses. A placement choice is made by determining which program can augment the youth's strengths while helping him cope with his problems. Many factors about the youth are considered before a placement choice is made; history of his behavior, how he related to professional staff in the unit, and his performance in the programs in which he participated while in the unit. An attempt is made to evaluate the underlying causes of his behavior and to choose a program which can deal with both the behavior and its underlying causes. In general, the Positive Peer Culture group modality is chosen unless a case can be made for placing a youth in the Intensive Treatment Program.

Objective 4: To arrange for transfer of wards to target units within three weeks.

The length of stay in the Intake Diagnostic Unit was available on 292 youth. The mean length of stay was 2.4 weeks. Most youth are placed in the Maxey "open program." Table 4.3.1 describes the placements made through the Intake Diagnostic Program.

TABLE 4.3.1

PLACEMENTS MADE BY INTAKE DIAGNOSTIC PROGRAM
Fiscal Year 1973-74

Placement	Number	Percent
Maxey Open Program	193	64.3
Green Oaks Center	67	22.3
Intensive Treatment Program	21	7.0
Adrian Training School	14	4.7
Other	5	1.7
TOTAL	300	100.0

4.3.2 The Intensive Treatment Program[5]

In theory, it has been convenient to classify problems of
youth into basically three large descriptive categories: (1) those
problems which are a function of specific, overt behavioral acts, or
youth classified as "social delinquents", (2) those problems which are
a function of internal personality dynamics, or youth classified as
neurotic, psychotic, or "emotionally disturbed", and (3) those problems which are a function of intelligence, or youth classified as
"retarded." Such theoretical classifications seldom, if ever, apply
to any specific personality and it is entirely probable for an individual youth to be retarded, emotionally disturbed and adjudicated a social delinquent, or to exhibit varying degrees of intensity within
these problem areas. Categorization of youth into these descriptive
classifications has tended to lend very little to either diagnosis,

---

[5]Placement data for youth processed through the Intake Program
during the months August and September 1973 was not available. Thus,
the placement data cited represents the last three quarters FY 73-74
and July 1973.

treatment or placement decisions especially when the youth required institutionalization. Where institutional placement has been required, it has historically been the procedure to place retarded and emotionally disturbed youth into institutions supported by the Department of Mental Health, and youth who are "socially delinquent" into institutions that are supported by the Department of Social Services such as Boys' and Girls' Training School programs.

Prior to 1963, youth who were diagnosed as retarded (i.e., an IQ under 70), or diagnosed as emotionally disturbed could be refused admittance to the Boys' Training School programs due to lack of appropriate programs for such youth. With the implementation of Public Act 229, no youth can be denied admittance to Boys' Training School programs based on his level of retardation or emotional stability, and provisions were made for the establishment of a unique program in Boys' Training School to deal with those youth who were adjudicated socially delinquent, but also exhibited a serious degree of emotional disturbance or retardation. This was referred to as the "F-Wing Program" which was located in the Reception Diagnostic Unit of the W. J. Maxey School at Whitmore Lake. This program had a capacity of twelve youth at any one time with a primary focus on intensive diagnosis and treatment to prepare a youth for future placement. The F-Wing Program was highly regarded for being capable of handling youth with these special problems.

With the implementation of the Decentralization Project, the Intensive Treatment Program was established as an expansion of the F-Wing Program to accommodate twenty youth at any given time.

Youth are referred to the Intensive Treatment Program either by the Intake Diagnostic Unit or prior to its closure, by the Crisis Intervention and Reassessment Unit. Intensive treatment provides a highly structured program with close staff supervision. The program provides both a diagnostic and treatment function. Youth remain in the program until they are able to move to a less supportive program which has a lower staff-to-youth ratio. The objectives of the Intensive Treatment Program are discussed in the sections that follow.

Objective 1: To provide alternative care for youth who require a more supportive environment which includes close and intensive involvement on a very personal basis to prepare these youth for release to a less supportive environment.

The Intensive Treatment Program has been established as a twenty-bed treatment program for youth who indicate high levels of "acute, pervasive and diffuse anxiety." Youth in the program can be hypersensitive, overracting, self-conscious, fearful, lacking in confidence, aggressive, or suffer from excessive guilt, remorse, and depression. According to staff, extreme flightiness and moodiness aimed at reducing immediate anxiety while ignoring long range consequences are typical of these youth. The overriding criteria for placement in the Intensive Treatment Program is that the rigorous personality and behavior dynamics of the youth, if placed in another program, would detract from treatment gains of other youth in that program and cause a disproportionate diversion of resources to deal with the intense nature of the individual youth's problems.

A total of 46 boys have been admitted to this program; 10 were from the community, seven from the Crisis Intervention and Reassessment Program, and 29 from the Intake Diagnostic Program.

Objective 2: To provide opportunities for youth to maintain contact with the community (including home visits).

A range of off-grounds activities included trips to the Detroit Zoo, Botanical Gardens, Metropolitan Airport and activities which provide some culturally enriching experiences. These activities are organized on both an individual and group basis. One to two off-grounds activities are planned each week and include such activities as bowling, ice skating, roller skating, movies, and church. Twice each month the group has a social program with a nearby college either at the college or at the training school. Each week the boys also go off-grounds to a local laundromat to wash their clothes.

Home visits are planned for boys when appropriate. Decisions

on when these visits occur are made individually for each youth but
each weekend at least one youth is scheduled for a home visit.
Families can also arrange to visit a youth at the training school.
These are planned on an individual basis.

Objective 3: To provide educational and recreational experiences for youth in the Intensive Treatment Program.

Each youth is involved in scheduled, constructive activities
which include an educational program, vocational arts, arts and crafts,
recreation, and religious programs.

Each week day the boys have scheduled academic and shop
classes followed by a schedule of recreational or off-grounds activities. These vary each day.

Objective 4: To provide therapeutic interaction through individual and group counseling and clinical treatment.

The basic treatment approach to youth in the Intensive Treatment Program is focused on saturating the youth's life with staff support, constructive activities and a therapeutic atmosphere where problematic behavior cannot be excused because the youth has problems.
"Normal," not problematic behavior is expected. Saturation by staff
support includes almost daily contact with two counselors, the program
administrator, two teachers, five boys supervisors, and depending on
the youth's schedule, contacts with management staff and several regularly scheduled groups from the community. While this requires the
youth to cope with several different persons over a given period of
time, this is a typical expectation of community life. The difference
is that staff tend to be much more thoroughly informed about the
youth's problems and what therapeutic behavior management techniques
are going to successfully meet the youth's needs.

The unit has available ten full-time staff plus supportive
services from seven other professional and line staff. This includes
the services of a psychologist and a psychiatrist.

Group counseling sessions are held once a week for all the boys
plus each counselor schedules sessions for his own group. The psychiatrist teaches a class related to specific problem areas one hour each
week. The counselors see boys individually throughout the week and the
psychologist and psychiatrist see boys on an individual basis as
necessary.

Objective 5: To transfer wards to less structured placements
within a period of six months.

The average length of stay for boys has been 6.1 months.
Forty boys were placed from the program in FY 1973-74. Of these, 20
were provided an institutional placement and 20 were assigned a community placement. See Table 4.3.2 for a distribution of placements.

TABLE 4.3.2

PLACEMENTS MADE BY INTENSIVE TREATMENT PROGRAM
Fiscal Year 1973-74

Placement	Number	Percent
Institutional Placements	20	50.0
Green Oaks Center	9	22.5
Maxey Open Program	3	7.5
Camps	7	17.5
Mental Health Facility	1	2.5
Community Placements	20	50.0
Halfway House	4	10.0
Foster Home	5	12.5
Own Home	11	27.5
TOTAL	40	100.0

4.3.3   Crisis Intervention and Reevaluation Program

The Crisis Intervention Unit was designed for (1) crisis management, and (2) reassessment of youth having adjustment difficulties
of an "acute or chronic" nature. The unit was opened in January 1972.

The crisis component handled up to 30 percent of the admissions; the reassessment component handled the other 70 percent. The Crisis Intervention and Reevaluation Unit was closed in March 1975, a decision based on the position that crisis and reassessment should be handled in the youth's residential unit, thereby avoiding the phenomenon of referring or "dumping" problem youth without really working to solve the problem in situ. Centers are now responsible for their youth and when necessary, may call on crisis staff for on site adjustment.

CHAPTER 5

RELATIVE EFFECTIVENESS AND COST-EFFECTIVENESS

The relative effectiveness and cost-effectiveness analysis which follows is the second such study undertaken with respect to the Decentralization effort. In substance, it is a continuation of the first study completed in 1973.[1] While the first year study focused on the outcomes of youth in the first three months after initial placement, the relatively small sample did not allow for analysis of some critical variables, notably sex and race, and was limited, naturally, to conclusions based on a very short period of time after placement. The current study benefits from a considerably expanded sample. Two stages in the analysis differentiate the current study from the previous effort. First, this analysis examines three-month outcomes as before, but we have eliminated from this study all youth who changed placement, thus neutralizing the fourth outcome dimension, change of placement. In so doing, we derived a clearer picture of the short-term effects of the placement modality on client groups. Second, we developed a modified computer program to allow examination of outcomes after six months in placement. For the six-month study, all outcome dimensions were utilized and all youth were studied. The six-month analysis provides an overview of the longer-term effects of the program and may offer a more realistic picture of program function.

5.1   Intake Process and Sex

For the purposes of the cost-effectiveness analyses the three intake groups are separated by sex. The analysis by sex will be presented in separate sections.

---

[1]Decentralization Project: Year-End Research and Evaluation Report, November 1973.

The Male Population: Three-Month Outcomes

The fiscal year 1972-73 analysis of short term outcomes of youth indicated that residence in the Intake Center was a fairly strong predictor of success in placement.   Youth who received Intake Center services were considerably more likely to experience positive outcomes during the three months following placement.   Further, it was noted that as the length of stay in the Intake Center increased, so did the likelihood of effective and cost-effective first placements.   For the male population, this finding is supported by the current data (see Table 5.1.1) but indicates that Intake Center services were significantly more effective only for those youth for whom extended Intake Center services, in excess of five weeks, have been provided.   For those males receiving shorter lengths of stay in the Intake Center, outcomes were of little significant difference.   It is significant to note, however, that the nature of the placements made for Intake Center youth are considerably less costly than placements made directly by intake staff located at the youth home and are similar in costs to placements made by the Court. This pattern assures that placements made for Intake Center youth are more cost-effective than those placed directly by intake staff and slightly more cost-effective than court placements.   This takes on added significance upon review of the demographics of court placed youth and directly placed youth: both groups are less aggressive in nature and proportionately more male and white.   Thus, although Intake Center youth are more difficult to place, they are being placed and served more effectively and cost-effectively.

The Female Population: Three-Month Outcomes

Among female youth, the most effective, least costly, and most cost-effective outcomes are achieved by girls placed, within five weeks, out of the Defer House intake facility.   The average costs for these females are considerably lower than for those with longer stays in the intake facility.   The females held longest in the Defer facility tend to be the most difficult-to-place youth, predominantly those who have high truancy rates.   As indicated earlier, over 40 percent of Defer

TABLE 5.1.1

THE RELATIVE EFFECTIVENESS AND COST-EFFECTIVENESS OF
VARIOUS INTAKE PROCESSES BY SEX BASED
ON THREE-MONTH OUTCOMES

Intake Process	Relative Effectiveness		Average Cost		Relative Cost Effectiveness	
	Male	Female	Male	Female	Male	Female
Intake Center Service						
$\leq$ 5 weeks	1.02	1.00	$2,252	$1,888	.86	1.00
> 5 weeks	1.17	.72	2,494	3,256	.88	.42
Direct Intake	1.05	.83	3,329	3,032	.60	.52
Court Placement	1.06	.85	2,245	2,300	.82	.70

TABLE 5.1.2

THE RELATIVE EFFECTIVENESS AND COST-EFFECTIVENESS OF
VARIOUS INTAKE PROCESSES BY SEX BASED
ON SIX-MONTH OUTCOMES

Intake Process	Relative Effectiveness		Average Cost 2nd 3 months		Relative Cost Effectiveness	
	Male	Female	Male	Female	Male	Female
Intake Center	1.14	1.04	$2,052	$2,193	1.01	.86
Direct Intake	1.08	.89	3,467	2,558	.57	.64
Court Placement	1.10	1.00	2,364	1,827	.85	1.00

intake youth truanted during the period under study.

The Male and Female Populations: Six-Month Outcomes

For six-month data, the effect of Intake Center services persists: youth, both males and females, are more likely to be achieving
effective outcomes six months after initial placement if they have received the intensive services of the Intake Center. Although the Intake Center category is not broken out by length of stay in intake, it
is likely that the longer length-of-stay youth remain the most effectively treated; this effect has been noted in two earlier effectiveness
analyses.

For females, a significant shift in cost-effectiveness is evident at six months -- court placed females are achieving the most cost-
effective outcomes. See Table 5.1.2.

5.2   Intake Process and Offense Class

The data suggests a strong interaction between offense class
and the intake process. Among youth placed in the Intake Center, 65.0
percent were classified as aggressive. Among youth placed by the Wayne
County Court, only 27.3 percent were aggressive. Of youth placed directly by intake staff, without benefit of extended Intake Center diagnosis and placement, 54.2 percent were aggressive. Thus, with respect
to offense class, a series of tacit decisions by intake staff and court
personnel are resulting in a subtle but generally consistent policy
with respect to the disposition of youth at the onset of the intake
process. These decisions result in the Intake Center making a disproportionate number of placements for aggressive youth. Among Intake
Center placed youth with shorter lengths of stay (less than or equal
to five weeks) roughly half were aggressive, while among those held
longer, 70 percent were in the aggressive classification. Thus, although constituting a small proportion of the total intake population,
the longest held Intake Center youth were the most effectively and
cost-effectively placed group of all intake youth, despite the fact
that they were predominantly in the aggressive offense class. See
Table 5.2.1.

The six-month outcome table (Table 5.2.2) takes a broader view of the intake process and offense class interaction. With six-month outcomes, we find that (1) aggressive youth continue to be the most effectively and cost-effectively treated, (2) aggressive males receiving Intake Center services are served less effectively than those receiving court placements but are treated as cost-effectively, and (3) among nonaggressive males, Intake Center youth are served most effectively and cost-effectively.

The six-month outcome table also indicates that among females, court placed youth are the most cost-effectively treated.

Analysis

The relative effectiveness and cost-effectiveness findings closely parallel those of last year. Among males, the longer lengths of stay at the Intake Center, i.e., in excess of five weeks, favor effective outcomes during the first three months of placement.

Offense class also appears to have a consistent impact on the effectiveness and cost-effectiveness of placement, especially in combination with intake history. The more aggressive youth are more effectively and more cost-effectively served. Table 5.2.2 indicates that the more aggressive youth tend to be placed in more structured and more costly institutional placements. However, these better outcomes for aggressive youth are not simply a function of their institutional placement; regardless of placement, the more aggressive youth are both more effectively and cost-effectively placed and treated. These results are especially true for aggressive youth with longer lengths of stay at the Intake Center.

While the effectiveness of directly placed and court placed youth was roughly equal to Intake Center serviced youth in general (see Table 5.1.1), the Intake Center achieved considerable economies with a generally more aggressive youth population, achieving near parity in costs with court placed youth while dealing with a higher concentration of aggressive youth (see Tables 5.1.1 and 5.2.2). Thus, the Intake

TABLE 5.2.1

RELATIVE EFFECTIVENSSS & COST-EFFECTIVENESS OF
VARIOUS LENGTHS OF STAY IN INTAKE CENTER BY
OFFENSE CLASS BASED ON 3-MONTH OUTCOMES

Intake Length of Stay and Offense Class	Relative Effectiveness		Average Cost		Relative Cost Effectiveness	
	Male	Female	Male	Female	Male	Female
≤5 weeks						
1-3 Nonaggressive	.82	.72	$2,325	$2,704	.65	.49
4-6 Aggressive	.97	.80	3,341	3,067	.53	.48
>5 weeks						
1-3 Nonaggressive	1.00	.63	1,833	3,256	1.00	.35
4-6 Aggressive	1.04	–	2,690	–	.71	–

TABLE 5.2.2

RELATIVE EFFECTIVENESS & COST-EFFECTIVENESS OF
VARIOUS INTAKE PROCESSES BY OFFENSE CLASS
BASED ON SIX-MONTH OUTCOMES

Intake Process and Offense	Relative Effectiveness		Average Cost 2nd 3 Months		Relative Cost Effectiveness	
	Male	Female	Male	Female	Male	Female
Intake Center Services						
1-3 Nonaggressive	1.00	.96	$1,543	$2,342	1.00	.63
4-6 Aggressive	1.11	–	2,188	–	.78	–
Direct Intake						
1-3 Nonaggressive	.90	.76	2,880	2,643	.48	.44
4-6 Aggressive	1.08	1.07	3,739	2,281	.50	.72
Court						
1-3 Nonaggressive	.88	.95	2,325	1,827	.58	.80
4-6 Aggressive	1.23	–	2,413	–	.78	–

Center placed youth were treated more cost-effectively than directly
placed youth, and slightly more cost-effectively than court placed
youth.

The less aggressive youth--those youth who commit primarily
offenses against self or minor offenses against property--respond less
to adjudication and subsequent placement than the more difficult youth.
These less aggressive youth, including youth who were charged with
"status offenses,"[2] may be less appropriate targets for the juvenile
justice system as it currently operates. (Proposed revisions in the
Michigan Juvenile Code reflect this concern.)

Conclusions

As noted on the abstract of the 1973-74 Decentralization Grant
Proposal, the Intake Center "is intended to refine the diagnostic and
treatment planning for newly committed wards, reduce the amount of time
wards are detained in the Wayne County Youth Home, and avoid unnecessary
referrals to institutions due to pressure for speedy removal by the
Court."

As we have observed, the process of placing wards out of the
Wayne County Youth Home has been altered through a three-phase intake
process, whereby the "quick-and-easy" placements are made by the Court,
and the more difficult youth placed out of the Youth Home by intake
staff. The most difficult-to-place youth--the aggressive, black males--
are receiving the disproportionate percentage of Intake Center services,
and are achieving, incidentally, a disproportionate number of community
placements. Although there is no evidence to suggest systematic bias
with respect to placement, it is clear that a beneficial effect is being achieved through differential intake and differential placement.
Youth who are considered the most difficult to place are achieving predominantly less-structured placements that are at least as effective

---

[2]Status offenses are those acts which are considered illegal
because of the age of the youth, e.g., truancy, incorrigibility. These
offenses, if committed by an adult, would not be subject to prosecution.

and a bit more cost-effective than the predominantly more structured placements made for the easy-to-place youth.

Among males, longer length of stay at the Intake Center generally assures more effective and cost-effective outcomes during the first three months after placement regardless of offense class. The less aggressive youth are treated slightly less effectively than the more aggressive youth; however, more effective treatment for aggressive youth is achieved at greater costs and lower cost-effectiveness.

Females are negatively affected by longer lengths of stay in the intake process, lending support to earlier observations on intake history for females, i.e., Defer House appears to be either: (1) holding more difficult cases for extended periods of time, or (2) adversely affecting youth who receive Defer services.

5.3   Intake Process and Initial Placement

We have observed that the intake process involves a subtle but effective screening process which skims off or "creams" the easiest-to-place youth early in the process, at the court level, while the progressively more difficult-to-place youth are left to the Intake Center staff for eventual disposition, either by direct placement out of the court youth home or by referral to the Intake Center for more prolonged preplacement diagnosis and services. Intake Center services, we should emphasize, in effect constitute a first placement for some of the most difficult-to-place youth. Table 5.3.1 indicates that the majority of Intake Center youth, those receiving community placements, represent the most cost-effective placements. The table further indicates that there is little within-group difference in effectiveness between community and institutional youth, and that cost-effectiveness is primarily a function of the actual costs of placement. Thus, perhaps the most significant finding with respect to intake and placement is the high degree to which the Intake Center services give the hard-to-place youth an opportunity to receive a noninstitutional placement. In addition, Intake Center services enable these youth to earn effectiveness levels which are equal to or better than the levels achieved by direct intake or court placed

TABLE 5.3.1

RELATIVE EFFECTIVENESS AND COST-EFFECTIVENESS OF
INTAKE PROCESSES BY INITIAL PLACEMENT BASED
ON THREE-MONTH OUTCOMES

Placement and Intake History	Relative Effectiveness	Average Cost	Relative Cost Effectiveness
Community			
Intake Center			
≤5 weeks	1.00	$1,081	1.00
>5 weeks	1.12	1,419	.85
Direct Intake	.96	1,319	.79
Court[a]	-	-	-
Institutional			
Intake Center			
≤5 weeks	1.05	3,470	.33
>5 weeks	1.03	3,547	.34
Direct Intake	1.02	3,542	.31
Court	1.04	2,289	.49

[a]Only one case.

youth, regardless of the type of placement received. There is considerable support for the view that the Intake Center acts not so much as a
diagnostic facility but as interim placement of last resort. This latter
function, though not intended in the original program plan, shows
promise as a means of "treatment" for youth for whom immediate placement elsewhere is difficult or impossible.

Among males, the long-term outcomes for intake and initial
placement indicate that there is a deterioration in the community placement - Intake Center combination. After six months in placement, the
distribution of effectiveness ratios for all combinations level off,
with the exception of Intake Center youth that received institutional
services. While the effectiveness ratios for intake serviced

TABLE 5.3.2

RELATIVE EFFECTIVENESS AND COST-EFFECTIVENESS OF INTAKE
PROCESSES BY INITIAL PLACEMENT BASED ON SIX-MONTH OUTCOMES

Placement and Intake History	Relative Effectiveness		Average Cost 2nd 3 Months		Relative Cost Effectiveness	
	Male	Female	Male	Female	Male	Female
Community						
Intake Center						
≤5 weeks	.84	.66	$1,351	$1,581	.68	.46
>5 weeks	.80	1.00	1,101	1,096	.79	1.00
Direct Intake	.82	.62	1,500	1,126	.60	.60
Court[a]	-	-	-	-	-	-
Institutional						
Intake Center						
≤5 weeks	.99		2,892		.37	
>5 weeks	1.14	.72	3,370	3,200	.37	.25
Direct Intake	.88	.76	3,671	3,243	.26	.26
Court	.89	.84	2,364	1,875	.41	.49

[a]Only one case.

institutional youth are high, the confidence levels are low (≤5 weeks confidence level = .52, > 5 weeks confidence level = .25), suggesting that no firm conclusions should be drawn. It is clear that the three-month elevated effectiveness of Intake Center youth placed in community programs is not apparent after six months. While community placements may not be more effective, they are only slightly less effective than institutional placements, and remain considerably more cost-effective.

Among females, the sample size is very small, and no significant patterns are evident with respect to effectiveness, although in terms of cost-effectiveness, community placements are from 1.3 to 5.5 times as cost-effective.

5.4   Initial Placement

The three-month outcome analysis of initial placement indicates that community placements, particularly own home placements, are the most effective and cost-effective. Group homes and halfway houses are less effective than institutional placements, reflecting the required participation in skill programs and the more intensely custodial nature of institutional facilities. As later analysis will indicate, the primary benefactors from institutional care are the most aggressive youth, who represent 72 percent of the state institutional population. The community placements remain the most cost-effective placements for all

TABLE 5.4

RELATIVE EFFECTIVENESS AND COST-EFFECTIVENESS OF INITIAL
PLACEMENTS BASED ON THREE-MONTH OUTCOMES

Initial Placement	Relative Effectiveness	Average Cost	Relative Cost Effectiveness
Community Placement			
Group Homes, Halfway Houses[a]	.88	$1,984	.16
Own home, relative's home, independent living, foster home[b]	1.00	365	1.00
Institutional Placement			
State and private institutions[c]	.97	3,344	.11

[a]Halfway house youth represent approximately 66 percent of this category, group homes, 34 percent.

[b]Own home placements represent approximately 75 percent of this category.

[c]State institutions represent approximately 61 percent of this institutional category, private institutions 36 percent, and camps approximately three percent.

72

youth. Table 5.4 demonstrates that placements which are less structured
are considerably less costly. Thus, community placements are 1.5 to 9.0
as cost-effective as placements in state and private institutions.

5.5   Initial Placement and Offense Class

        Initial placement offers an interesting pattern with respect
to offense class. As in our earlier findings (FY 1972-73, p. 24),
aggressive youth are receiving more effective treatment than nonaggressive youth, within each type of placement. Unlike the previous analysis,
current data provides for a breakdown by male and female populations.
The refinement of the analysis, coupled with the concentration on youth
remaining in one placement, offers a new insight (see Table 5.5.1).

        Among males, it is evident that differences in effectiveness
are less a factor of placement than of level of aggressiveness. The
more aggressive youth are more effectively treated within each placement type, but the differences in effectiveness between placements is
not significant. Costs for institutional youth and community youth
differ considerably, as expected, but we find a considerable increase
in institutional costs as a function of a more aggressive offense history. The less aggressive institutionally placed youth are receiving
predominantly private institutional placements, as indicated by the
average cost of $29.42 per day. This group of youth is achieving less
effective outcomes than the more aggressive youth, with slightly higher
cost effectiveness due to the considerably lower cost. It is relatively safe to assume that this less aggressive institutionally placed youth
is a product of the court or direct intake processes.

        Among females, there are few community placements with aggres-
sive offense histories.[3] Nonaggressive females are placed with slightly
more effective outcomes in the community, at less than half the cost
of their institutionalized counterparts and with more than twice the
level of cost-effectiveness.

_____

        [3]For the three month outcomes, the four females in this category
were omitted from the analysis by the computer.

TABLE 5.5.1

RELATIVE EFFECTIVENESS AND COST-EFFECTIVENESS OF INITIAL
PLACEMENT BY OFFENSE CLASS BASED ON THREE-MONTH OUTCOMES

Type of Placement and Offense Class	Relative Effectiveness		Average Cost		Relative Cost Effectiveness	
	Male	Female	Male	Female	Male	Female
Community						
1-3 Nonaggressive	.81	.74	$1,166	$1,280	.99	.80
4-6 Aggressive	1.00	-	1,375	-	1.00	-
Institution						
1-3 Nonaggressive	.86	.71	2,648	3,288	.45	.30
4-6 Aggressive	1.00	.81	3,680	3,777	.37	.29

TABLE 5.5.2

RELATIVE EFFECTIVENESS AND COST-EFFECTIVENESS OF INITIAL
PLACEMENT BY OFFENSE CLASS BASED ON SIX-MONTH OUTCOMES

Type of Placement and Offense Class	Relative Effectiveness		Average Cost 2nd 3 Months		Relative Cost Effectiveness	
	Male	Female	Male	Female	Male	Female
Community						
1-3 Nonaggressive	1.04	.93	$1,034	$1,442	.45	.29
4-6 Aggressive	1.14	1.00	1,361	449	.38	1.00
Institution						
1-3 Nonaggressive	1.08	1.02	2,906	2,880	.17	.16
4-6 Aggressive	1.32	1.44	3,523	3,398	.17	.19

The six-month outcomes demonstrate remarkable stability over
time in the relationships between initial placement and offense class.
For males in particular, high aggressiveness plays the significant role

in the determination of effective placement, in both community and
institutional settings. While there is no direct proof, the persis-
tence of this phenomenon coupled with the high proportion of aggressive
youth placed out of the Intake Center suggests that the Intake Center
services may be one factor contributing to the relative success of the
more aggressive youth, although it certainly explains only a portion of
the phenomenon. As was indicated in our earlier discussion on intake
process and offense class, aggressive youth achieve more effective
three-month and six-month outcomes regardless of intake procedure.
Still, unlike other intake subpopulations, the majority of youth receiving Intake Center services are aggressive youth.

5.6   Age of Admission and Offense Class

The Male Population

Among males, greatest effectiveness was achieved among the
youth admitted earlier with most aggressive offense histories. These
youth appear to be served more effectively, albeit more expensively, in
higher structure placements. This finding supports last year's finding
(Fiscal Year 1972-73, Table 19), that youth admitted early to an institution are relatively more responsive than older youth to institutional
programs. The latest findings clarify this point by demonstrating that
it is the highly aggressive, younger youth who is the most likely to
benefit from institutional placement; the nonaggressive youth is less
likely to be a recipient of institutional placement, particularly youth
adjudicated prior to age 15. Male nonaggressive youth, subjected to
adjudication and placement at an older age, are the most likely to receive community placements and be treated most effectively and cost-
effectively.

Section 3.1   indicates that the more aggressive offenses are
being committed by youth who are older at age of admission. The effectiveness study indicates that these older, more aggressive youth are
less likely than their younger counterparts to achieve effective and
cost-effective outcomes. While our analysis suggests that aggressive
youth achieve similarly effective treatment, regardless of placement,

community placements for these youth are about 2.5 times as cost-effective as institutional placements. Among males with lower aggressiveness, early adjudication appears inadvisable; these youth are generally younger, are least effectively treated when admitted early, and are the most likely to "self-correct" within the community. This finding supports the finding in fiscal year 1972-73,to wit: that longer delay before admission, particularly for the less aggressive youth, is most likely to result in effective treatment. Early adjudication does not allow the younger, marginally delinquent youth sufficient time to correct his behavior problems through self-adjustment. This is evidence that youth admitted before age 14 are not only more costly to treat, but they are least likely to achieve positive outcomes.[4]

The Female Population

Among females, the least costly and most highly effective and cost-effective placements were provided to the older, aggressive offenders. These girls represented 8.5 percent of the total female population, and, by virtue of their cost, are presumed to be halfway house community placements. Similarly, the younger, aggressive youth represented 11.0 percent of the total female population. They are the most expensive and least cost-effective to treat among both males and females. The younger, aggressive youth are receiving primarily institutional placements. In summary, the more aggressive females represent only 20 percent of the female ward population, and are placed differentially. The older girls are placed in community placements or private institutions, where they are treated most effectively and most cost-effectively while the younger aggressive females are placed institutionally and are average in effectiveness and least cost-effective. The indications from this admittedly small sample suggest that the more aggressive female would most wisely be placed in community placements or private institutions regardless of age. The relative success of

---

[4]Fiscal year 1972-73 report, p. 26.

76

the older females in these placements, with respect to both effectiveness and cost-effectiveness, argues strongly for a different placement strategy for aggressive females, and suggests an area for further study.

The greatest proportion of the females are nonaggressive (80 percent). Unlike the males, earlier admission is consistently more favorable to effective and cost-effective placement. From the cost figures, we may presume a high representation of these youth among community placements.

TABLE 5.6

RELATIVE EFFECTIVENESS AND COST-EFFECTIVENESS OF VARIOUS
AGES-AT-ADMISSION AND OFFENSE CLASS COMBINATIONS
BASED ON THREE-MONTH OUTCOMES

Age at Admission and Offense Class	Relative Effectiveness		Average Cost		Relative Cost Effectiveness	
	Male	Female	Male	Female	Male	Female
<15.5 Nonaggressive	.75	.77	$2,107	$2,749	.88	.69
Aggressive	1.07	.80	3,190	3,720	.84	.53
>15.5 Nonaggressive	1.00	.70	2,483	2,788	1.00	.62
Aggressive	.96	.85	3,255	2,153	.73	.97

5.7   Delay and Age of Admission

A 12-24 month delay between age of first offense and age of admission is most effective among both males and females with either earlier or later ages at admission. The effect of delay on effectiveness as a function of age is noted at the extremes in delay: Among youth admitted at an earlier age, short delays are least effective; among youth admitted in the later age range, longest delays are least effective. Thus, we may conclude that youth admitted at the extremes in age are likely to be less effectively treated.

TABLE 5.7

RELATIVE EFFECTIVENESS AND COST-EFFECTIVENESS OF VARIOUS
DELAY AND AGE-AT-ADMISSION COMBINATION
BASED ON THREE-MONTH OUTCOMES

Age of Admission and Delay	Relative Effectiveness		Average Cost		Relative Cost Effectiveness	
	Male	Female	Male	Female	Male	Female
15.5 years						
<12 mos.	1.00	.83	$2,422	$2,700	1.00	.74
12-24 mos.	1.14	.99	3,161	3,274	.87	.73
>24 mos.	1.12	.85	2,596	3,070	.92	.69
15.5 years						
<12 mos.	1.07	.80	2,942	2,710	.88	.71
12-24 mos.	1.17	.90	3,017	2,846	.94	.77
>24 mos.	1.02	.74	3,140	2,324	.79	.77

5.8   Offense Class and Delay

For both males and females, the most successful or more effective treatment is provided for youth who are in the 12-24 month delay category. This trend supports the findings with respect to delay that were noted in the correlation of delay and age at admission, i.e., that the extremes in delay, less than 12 months or more than 24 months, are less likely to result in positive outcomes for youth. One can only speculate on the reasons for this trend, since the findings are not totally consistent with last year's observation, which suggested that longest delays were most effective. The current findings are especially interesting in that there is consistency across sex, ages of admission, and levels of aggressiveness. Cost figures indicate that the 12-24 month delay results in slightly more costly placements, and that these placements generally are more effective.

TABLE 5.8

RELATIVE EFFECTIVENESS AND COST-EFFECTIVENESS OF VARIOUS
OFFENSE CLASS AND DELAY COMBINATIONS
BASED ON THREE-MONTH OUTCOMES

Offense Class and Delay	Relative Effectiveness		Average Cost		Relative Cost Effectiveness	
	Male	Female	Male	Female	Male	Female
1-3 Nonaggressive						
12 mos. or less	.86	.74	$2,266	$2,736	.91	.65
12-24 mos.	1.00	.86	2,419	2,991	1.00	.69
24 mos.+	.82	.68	2,079	2,567	.96	.65
4-6 Aggressive						
12 mos. or less	1.01	.79	2,904	2,540	.84	.75
12-24 mos.	1.11		3,438		.78	
24 mos.+	1.04	.83	3,314	3,230	.76	.62

CHAPTER 6

CONCLUSIONS AND POLICY IMPLICATIONS

This report has focused primarily on the Decentralization Project and the analysis of intake and client characteristics within the youth services system operating in Wayne County. Some care should be exercised in the extrapolation and application of Wayne County intake and demographic data to counties outside the Detroit Metropolitan area. On the other hand, Wayne County accounts for some forty percent of Michigan's delinquent state wards. In examining the Decentralization Project, we have examined not only a considerable proportion of all state wards, but have assessed the prevailing treatment policy of the Michigan Department of Social Services, a policy which stresses an individualized treatment plan and the provision of placement services which best meet the needs of the delinquent state ward. This policy, termed "planned differential placement," is the intended focus of the decentralization concept.

The commitment of the Department of Social Services to offer planned differential placement to delinquent and troubled youth is reflected in the state's commitment of funds to those services that formerly were funded by the Law Enforcement Assistance Administration under the rubric of "Decentralization." As a philosophy, decentralization has been broadened to include the entire breadth of services to delinquent youth in the State of Michigan. This evaluation has attempted to reflect a broad overview of not only the components of the decentralization process in Wayne County, but also the implications of the decentralization effort for differential placement, differential intake, community residential care programs, institutional programs, and ancillary decentralization components, such as attention centers.

Differential Placement

As we have demonstrated, the intake process in Wayne County effects differential placements for some youth--specifically, those

youth who have been sorted out, albeit incompletely, by the court intake
placement process and the Intake Center placement process. The path
that a youth follows through the initial stages of the juvenile justice
system is determined, at least in part, by the differentiation of youth
on the basis of race, sex, offense class, and to a lesser extent, the
additional variables noted in the demographic analysis. Although the
evaluation has demonstrated a tacit process of differential placement,
there is considerable anecdotal evidence that less than rational decision rules are contributing significantly to the placement process.

One of the most cogent decision factors regarding placement
might be termed the "bed space rule." Intake workers are limited considerably in the execution of ideal placements by the unavailability of
the desired placement. At almost every level in the placement system,
in varying degrees, the potential placements--the "receivers" of youth--
establish criteria which limit the type of youth that they will handle.
Thus, for certain "types" of youth, securing placement alternatives is
more difficult. Generally, these youth are retained in the Intake
Center until appropriate placement can be arranged. As we have noted,
this process can take as long as six months.

A paradoxical aspect of this phenomenon evidences itself in
the consistent underutilization of community placements, particularly
the halfway houses, which generally operate at less than full capacity.
It is not fully understood whether this underutilization is (1) a
function of the normal process of deselection of less desirable youth,
(2) a reflection of structural underutilization due to placement turn-
over, (3) an indication of an inefficient communications network, or
(4) a combination of these factors. Nonetheless, amelioration of this
phenomenon is necessary before expanded community placements in Wayne
County can be justified.

Thus, while differential placement is clearly taking place,
it is not clear that it is working as intended. The effect of the intake process on "deselecting" youth, with the eventual disposition of
substantial numbers of the more aggressive Intake Center serviced youth

into community placements, is a clear example of differential placement. There is considerable prima facie merit to this process, particularly in light of the findings indicating relatively effective and cost-effective outcomes in placement for some of the most aggressive and difficult-to-place youth. It is questionable, however, whether the deselection process currently operating is ideal, since it tends to channel the less aggressive youth into institutions and the more aggressive youth into community placements. While it may be pragmatic for the court to continue selecting and placing white nonaggressive males in private institutions, the court placed youth may actually be more appropriate candidates for community placement. Similarly, the aggressive community placed youth might be better served by the more structured facilities offered in the private sector. Of the directly placed youth, who receive primarily state institutional placement, the less aggressive may more likely be candidates for community placement. Thus, crucial questions remain: Why are the most aggressive youth receiving predominately community placements? Is their relative success in the community an indication of the special suitability of community based services to the more aggressive youth, or does it indicate simply that the community can serve aggressive youth equally as well as the institutions? More critically, are we making the most efficient use of the institutions, which would appear to be more suited for the more aggressive youth? These questions raise issues that must be addressed within the context of the juvenile justice system as it now operates, but they also can be brought to bear on proposed changes in the system. Specifically, the consistently lower degree of responsiveness to treatment evidenced by the less aggressive youth, regardless of placement, suggests that a portion of the less aggressive population--the "incorrigibles" and truants (status offenders) may not be appropriate targets for court and Department of Social Services intervention.

The stigma attached to the court's labeling of a youth as "pre-delinquent" or "delinquent" certainly can have only negative impact on the youths self-image. The fairness of court and state intervention into a status offender's life is questionable at best. In light of the apparent failure of such intervention, it clearly behooves the courts, the Legislature, and the providers of services to either eliminate the intervention or provide intervention that effectively meets the youth's needs.

Placement Alternatives

The placement alternatives available throughout the state system offer a wide range of services, and as we have noted, serve youth with varying degrees of effectiveness and cost-effectiveness.

The state training schools at Whitmore Lake and Adrian have demonstrated some success in reducing truancy and providing educational services to youth in placement. Although there are no walls, the institutions have adopted an aggressive approach to containment of youth. During a youth's containment, he or she must participate in the programs offered at the institution. In a sense, the institutional programs are relatively fail-safe with respect to in-program outcomes--the youth have no choice but to participate. Within this framework, the relative "success" of in-program outcomes is guaranteed, and the effectiveness measures are inflated accordingly. To more accurately determine the relative effectiveness of institutional programs, matched or similar youth from institutional and community programs must be assessed after release from their respective programs to determine the relative long-term impacts of state and private institutional and community placement-treatment modalities. This type of research has been undertaken, with results expected in 1976.

It is clear that state institutional programs are providing necessary services, particularly to the most aggressive and disturbed male youth, through programs such as the Maxey Intensive Treatment program. The relative success of institutional placements with the less aggressive youth is more clearly an effect of the private institutional and camp placement programs, which constitute 39 percent of all "institutional placements." As noted earlier, private institutional and camp placements are primarily the domain of the white, nonaggressive youth. Of white youth, 29 percent are placed in Maxey or Adrian

Training Schools; for black youth, 54 percent are placed in the state training schools. Thus, although blacks are achieving predominantly community placements, those who are institutionalized are most heavily represented in the state-operated training schools.

Community programs allied with the Decentralization Project have had considerable success if one takes into account the relative aggressiveness of the community placements. The Intake Center has succeeded in placing the most difficult-to-place youth in community placements and achieved effective and particularly cost-effective outcomes. Our analysis indicates that these community placements appear to deteriorate in effectiveness somewhat between the third and sixth month of placement. However, this effect is doubtless aggravated by the earlier release of the most successful community youth and the concomitant increase, at around six months, in the proportion of "difficult" youth remaining in the community population.

The attention center programs have been effective in providing short-term services to community placed youth, particularly those in interim placements at Defer Place or the Intake Center, although the truancy rates at both facilities are sufficiently high to mitigate the effectiveness of the services offered. In addition, there is some evidence that the attention centers are reaching a population that would be unlikely candidates for traditional skill, educational, and recreational programs. The study of the attention centers raises the issue of whether the centers are providing services for a sufficient length of time to result in a meaningful impact on the target population. A more rigorous evaluation and screening process before selection and referral to the attention centers might assist the centers in enlisting a more suitable client population and in more effectively allocating services and resources.

It has become clear that both institutional and community services are offering positive short-term intervention for delinquents by way of providing counseling and educational services in varying degrees. The institutional components, with more structured programs,

appear most suitable for the most disturbed and intractable youth. It
is not evident from our data that these youth constitute the primary
client population of the institutions. Similarly, the less aggressive
youth, who may be more amenable to community placement are in many cases
receiving institutional placement, particularly in private institutions.

Discussion

The success of decentralization as a process resides in the
program's demonstration that alternatives to institutionalization are
indeed viable avenues of approach to the deep-seated and growing problems associated with juvenile delinquency and the criminal justice
system. The project has fostered increasing cooperation between institutional and community services personnel and has paved the way for the
introduction of numerous ancillary services outside of the traditional
institutional setting. Institutional administrators point to a development within their organizations of a greater focus on the more disturbed youth. It is presumed that at least part of this trend is a
function of the selective placement of youth for whom institutionalization is deemed most likely effective. As has been noted earlier, the
differential placement concept is stronger in its intent than in its
application; internal management difficulties inherent in the nature of
the juvenile justice system, e.g., the competition for clients who are
more manageable, the natural inclinations of houseparents to vie for
specific types of youth, and the inequities of the courts in the adjustment of cases among the well-to-do, are realities which are not easily
legislated or managed away.

In addition, we have noted the difficulties in serving an extremely heterogeneous delinquent population. The client population
ranges from the most severe social deviants who have histories of griev-
ous assaults, to the troubled youth chronically truant from unbearable
family situations. Currently, both groups fall under a uniform juvenile code which in its application often affects youth similarly, though
their needs differ considerably. This system must be refined through
court, legislative, and service agency action to (1) set boundaries on

the scope of juvenile delinquency; (2) clarify the role of the courts and social service agencies in meeting the needs of society and the offender; and (3) establish accountability for rehabilitation of the various classes of offenders.

At least two steps are necessary for the full implementation of the planned differential placement concept. First, there must be a recognition on the part of administrative staff that inequities now exist. The Wayne County Court placement policy for state wards should be subjected to a critical examination to determine (1) why the court exercises bias with respect to client and placement type; and (2) whether the Department of Social Services should remain accountable for youth committed to the state but not placed according to departmental plan. Second, the Department of Social Services must establish an increasingly clearer policy with respect to placement philosophy by incorporating internal and external research findings to develop more specific guidelines for differential placement. Intake and placement personnel should be educated with the intent of fostering a commitment to insure the most appropriate intervention in a youth's destructive life pattern.

As stated above, these observations are in no way intended to derogate the services now provided and the staff involved; rather, they are viewed as a direction toward constructive change. The decentralization concept has demonstrated the feasibility and desirability of decentralized intake and placement. As the decentralization concept is expanded, every effort should be made to insure increasing organizational adherence to the goal of rational, planned differential placement.

APPENDICES

APPENDIX A

Principle Component Analysis and the Combined Outcome Scale

One major task in utilizing an effectiveness and cost-effective-ness model in the study of delinquency treatment is the creation of a unit outcome which reliably and validly reflects the impact of treatment upon individual youth. The unit outcome which reflects the impact of delinquency treatment should satisfy certain criteria. First, because delinquency treatment is being evaluated, the unit outcome should reflect the relative social utility of each outcome category. The relative social utility of the outcome categories was determined through staff analysis and ranking of the categories according to their value as indicators of success or failure in programs. Second, in order to discriminate between youths, the unit outcome must reflect as much variability as possible.

Table A-1 lists the outcome parameters, on which each youth was assessed. The simplest mathematical technique for combining these four outcomes is a linear combination:

$$0 = a_1 \, 0_1 + a_2 \, 0_2 + a_3 \, 0_3 + a_4 \, 0_4$$

The signs of the coefficients of a's should be chosen so as to be consistent in terms of increasing (or decreasing) "social utility." These values should reflect the relative importance of the four variables. If we interpret "relative importance" to be similar to "ability to discriminate between youths" we look for a linear combination which has as much variability as possible under some normalizing constraint, e.g., $\Sigma \, a_i^2 = 1$, where the sum of the squares will equal 1.

The appropriate multivariate technique is called principle components. In this case, the first principle component, with values a_1, a_2, a_3, and a_4, explained 90.0 percent of the total population variation. Fortunately, the sign criteria was also met; the values were all positive.

TABLE A-1

OUTCOME EVALUATION CATEGORIES

Outcome Category	Rank Order Ranges	Social Utility Weighting (principle component values)
Education	1-3	$a_1 = .2224$
Employment	1-3	$a_2 = .2992$
Recidivism	1-13	$a_3 = .8089$
Placement	1-5	$a_4 = .4547$

Since the principle component weights supported the staff assessment of social utility, and since all the criteria were met, this technique for data reduction was considered appropriate.

DECENTRALIZATION QUARTERLY REPORT
(Please record information as indicated. Record remarks on back of sheet.)

DATE OF REPORT _____

NAME OF CASEWORKER _____

NAME OF YOUTH _____

DO NOT WRITE IN THIS AREA

1. Record current PLACEMENT on the appropriate line and give dates for any PLACEMENT CHANGES and FACILITY CHANGES made within quarter.

	Month	Day	Facility #	Facilities:
0. Adult correctional facility	____	____	_____	1. Training school
1. Community placement (Module 3)	____	____	_____	2. Camp
2. Institutional placement (Module 4)	____	____	_____	3. Private institution
3. Placed in community after				(name) _____
institutional placement (Module 5)	____	____	_____	4. Own home

If youth changed placement during quarter, note direction of change:

5. Relative's home
6. Foster home

4. Module 3 to Module 4 (community to institution) ____ ____ _____ 7. Independent living
5. Module 5 to Module 4 (reinstitutionalized) ____ ____ _____ 8. Group home
                                                                  9. Halfway house
6. Module 4 to Module 5 status (institution to community) ____ ____ _____ 10. _____
7. No change ____ ____ _____

2. During the quarter, did the youth participate in an EDUCATIONAL PROGRAM? If NO, place a (1) in this box ( ). If YES, record dates and program numbers on the appropriate lines.

	Month	Day	Program #	Programs:
2. Began program	____	____	_____	1. Public school
3. Completed program (H.S. diploma or GED)	____	____	_____	2. GED
4. Terminated unsuccessfully	____	____	_____	3. Pre-GED
5. Terminated due to placement change	____	____	_____	4. Special Ed.
6. Continued program, progress satisfactory			_____	5. Other
7. Continued program, progress or attendance poor			_____	

3. During the quarter, did the youth participate in an EMPLOYMENT PROGRAM? If NO, place a (1) in this box ( ). If YES, record dates and program numbers on the appropriate lines.

	Month	Day	Program #	Programs:
2. Began employment	____	____	_____	1. Subsidized work experience within placement
3. Terminated unsuccessfully	____	____	_____	
4. Terminated, participation satisfactory	____	____	_____	2. N.Y.C. or other outside subsidized employment
5. Continued employment			_____	

If the youth is actively seeking employment individually or through job placement services, place a (6) in this box ( ).

3. Outside employment, part-time
4. Outside employment, full-time
5. Other _____

4. During the quarter, did the youth participate in VOCATIONAL TRAINING? If NO, place a (1) in the box ( ). If YES, record dates on the appropriate lines and specify name of program.

	Month	Day	Program
2. Began program	____	____	_____
3. Completed program	____	____	_____
4. Terminated unsuccessfully	____	____	_____
5. Terminated due to placement change	____	____	_____
6. Continued program	____	____	_____

5. Has the youth ever participated in an ATTENTION CENTER? If NO, place a (1) in the box ( ). If YES, record status on the appropriate lines and give date if within the quarter.

	Month	Day	Center #	Center:
2. Began program	____	____	_____	1. Eastside
3. Completed program	____	____	_____	2. Westside
4. Terminated unsuccessfully	____	____	_____	
5. Terminated due to placement change	____	____	_____	
6. Continued program			_____	

6. Was youth TRUANT during the quarter? If NO, place a (1) in the box ( ). If YES, check category for total length of time youth was truant.

2. _____ 1 to 5 days
3. _____ 6 to 14 days
4. _____ 2 to 4 weeks
5. _____ 1 to 2 months
6. _____ 2 to 3 months

7. During the quarter, did youth have any POLICE CONTACTS (not resulting in arrest, and for reasons other than truancy?

1. _____ No
2. _____ Yes

8. Was youth ARRESTED during quarter? If NO, place a (1) in the box ( ). If YES, record nature of offense(s), date(s), and outcome(s).

Nature of Offense	Month	Day	Outcome	Outcomes:
_____	____	____	____	2. Returned to prior placement
_____	____	____	____	3. Given other community placement
_____	____	____	____	4. Placed in institution
				5. Under jurisdiction of adult court
				6. Outcome not yet determined

DSS-3348 (Rev. 10-73) Previous edition obsolete.

APPENDIX B

THE WAYNE COUNTY DELINQUENT STATE WARD:
A DEMOGRAPHIC PROFILE

This appendix describes the demographic composition of the delinquent state ward population. This description encompasses five major demographic variables described in the methodology, plus an additional variable, delay, calculated from two of the original demographic variables. Again, they include sex, race, level of aggressiveness or offense class, age at first offense, age of admission, and delay. A brief summary of this analysis is presented in Chapter 3.

B-1   Race and Sex

The state ward population is predominantly black and male. Males compose approximately 75 percent of the population. About 60 percent of the population is black. Chi-square analysis indicates that race and sex are highly dependent attributes ($\rho > .999$). See Table B-1.

B-2   Level of Aggressiveness

The frequency of youth within each level of aggressiveness is highly variable. Aggressive offenses, levels 4-6, comprise 55 percent of all offenses, whereas nonaggressive acts constitute the remaining 45 percent.

A more meaningful perspective of the level-of-aggressiveness continuum can be obtained by combining conceptually distinct aggressiveness levels. An operational set of three aggressiveness categories is created by pooling all nonaggressive acts (levels 1-3), all aggressive acts that are not physically injurious (levels 4-5) and all aggressive acts that are physically injurious (level 6). Youths committing nonaggressive acts account for about 45 percent, aggressive and noninjurious acts for 25 percent, and aggressive and injurious acts for 30 percent of the total sample.

B-2.1   Level of Aggressiveness and Sex

The data strongly suggests that the aggressiveness level is dependent upon the aggressor's sex. In fact, males commit approximately four times as many aggressive offenses as females, whereas females commit two and one-half times as many nonaggressive offenses as males. Chi-square analysis strongly supports the hypothesis of dependence between sex and the level of aggressiveness ($\rho > .999$). See Table B-2.1.

B-2.2   Level of Aggressiveness and Race

The data indicates that race and level of aggressiveness are interdependent ($\rho > .999$). Among black youth, 62 percent have histories of aggressive offenses; 40 percent are aggressive and injurious. Among white youth only 35 percent have aggressive offense histories; 18 percent are aggressive and injurious. See Table B-2.2.

B-2.3   Level of Aggressiveness, Race, and Sex

A three-way analysis of aggressiveness, race and sex indicates, as expected, that the three attributes are interdependent ($\rho > .999$). Black males have more severe offense histories, with 47 percent classified as aggressive and injurious. Among white males, 22 percent were placed in this category. Among females, the frequency of blacks classified as aggressive is about three times the frequency of whites. Table B-2.3.

B-2.4   Summary: Level of Aggressiveness

Black males comprise 44 percent of the population and commit a majority of the aggressive offenses. White males constitute 32 percent of the population and commit a predominance of aggressive offenses, though not with the frequency and severity of black males. Black females compose 14 percent of the population and commit primarily nonaggressive acts; 79 percent of these females are nonaggressive. White females constitute 10 percent of the population; 93 percent of all them are nonaggressive.

B-3   Age at First Offense

Age at first offense is the date of a youth's first officially recorded violation of the juvenile or adult legal code. Mean age at first offense was 13.6 years and ranged from seven to sixteen years. Surprisingly, almost 20 percent of the youths were eleven years old or younger when they committed their first offense. However, for the majority of youth, age at first offense is between thirteen and fifteen years. See Figure B-3.

To facilitate the analysis of complex interactions, age at first offense will be collapsed into the three age groups listed below:

Group 1:   Youth less than or equal to twelve years of age ($\leq$ 12.0);

Group 2:   Youth older than twelve and less than or equal to fourteen years (12.1 through 14.0);

Group 3:   Youth older than fourteen years (> 14.0).

B-3.1   Age at First Offense and Sex

Recorded instances of delinquent behavior for males commences at a younger age than it does for females. Mean age at first offense for males is 11.7 years, while for females it is 12.3 years. See Table B-3.1 and Figure B-3.1.

B-3.2   Age at First Offense and Race

In general, race is not highly correlated with age of first offense, although blacks commence offense behavior, on the average, at a younger age than whites. Mean age at first offense for blacks is 11.6 years and for whites it is 12.3 years. Twenty-six percent of the white population commit their first offense on or before the age of twelve, whereas for black youth, 34 percent have committed their first offense by this age. Chi-square analysis indicates a slight trend towards dependence; however, it is not statistically significant ($.80 \leq \rho \leq .90$). See Table B-3.2.

B-3.3   Age at First Offense and Level of Aggressiveness

If a youth commits his first offense on or before the age of twelve, there is a greater likelihood for the youth to commit an aggressive offense than there is for youth whose initial offense occurred after the age of twelve years. Forty percent of the aggressive and injurious youth committed their first offense on or before the age of 12, as did 35 percent of the aggressive and noninjurious youth. Only 23 percent of the nonaggressive youth committed their first offense before the age of 12. See Table B-3.3 and Figure B-3.3.

B-3.4   Summary: Age at First Offense

Two salient points emerge from the analysis of age at first offense. First, males tend to commit their first offense at a younger age than females. Second, the younger the age at first offense, the greater the probability that subsequent offenses will be aggressive.

B-4   Age at Admission

Mean age at admission to state wardship is 15.6 years. (See Figure B-4.) To again facilitate the analysis of complex interactions, age of admission will be collapsed into three groups. The age ranges of the three groups are as follows:

Group 1:   less than or equal to fourteen years ($\leq$ 14.0)

Group 2:   greater than fourteen and less than or equal to sixteen years (14.1-16.0)

Group 3:   greater than sixteen years ($\geq$ 16.0)

B-4.1   Age at Admission and Sex

A larger proportion of females than males are adjudicated on or before the age of fourteen. However, this factor does not produce any major overall differences in the age of admission between the sexes. Mean age at admission for females is 15.4 years and for males if 15.3 years. Hence, age at admission is not affected significantly by the sex of the youth. See Table B-4.1.

B-4.2   Age at Admission and Race

Age at admission and race are statistically independent attributes. Frequency distributions for white and black youth are almost
identical across the collapsed categories of age at admission. That
is, within-group frequencies are approximately equal for white and
black youth. Chi-square analysis supports this hypothesis of indepen-
dence (.50 < ρ < .70). See Table B-4.2.

B-4.3   Age at Admission and Level of Aggressiveness

The data suggests that age at admission and the level of aggressiveness are statistically dependent attributes. In general, the
more aggressive offenses are being committed by older youth. Forty-
eight percent of all aggressive and injurious youth were older than 16
years at admission. Moreover, 42 percent of all aggressive and noninjurious youth were in the same age group at admission. However, 71
percent of the youth adjudicated for nonaggressive offenses were 16
years of age or under when they were admitted to state wardship.
Figure B-4.3 demonstrates this relationship quite clearly. Finally,
chi-square analysis supports this hypothesis of dependence between
age of admission and the level of aggressiveness (.975 < ρ < .999).
See Table B-4.3 and Figure B-4.3.

B-4.4   Age at Admission and Age at First Offense

In general, the younger the youth at the time of his first
offense, the more likely the youth will be adjudicated at a younger
age. This relationship is to a large degree a result of operational
definition; it is a rare case for young people to be adjudicated before
they commit any offenses. Chi-square analysis does support this dependence (ρ > .999); however, from a researcher's perspective, the
significance must be viewed more as an artifact of design than as a
crucial behavioral event. See Table B-4.4.

B-4.5   Summary: Age at Admission

Excluding age at first offense for reasons mentioned above,

level of aggressiveness is the only variable to be significantly dependent with age at admission. In general, the older the youth at admission the greater the likelihood that this youth was adjudicated for committing an aggressive offense. Conversely, the younger the youth at admission the greater the likelihood the youth has committed a non-aggressive offense.

B-5   Delay

Delay is the amount of time between a youth's first officially recorded offense and his subsequent adjudication to state wardship. The mean period of delay for the sample is 21.6 months. This mean should be viewed with caution, however, because the statistic is quite variable; its standard deviation is 17.8 months.

To simplify the analysis, delay will also be collapsed into three groups. They are presented below:

Delay Group 1: 1-18 months
Delay Group 2: 19-36 months
Delay Group 3: 37+ months

B-5.1   Delay and Sex

The data indicates that delay and sex have a dependent tendency. Females generally experience a shorter delay than males. In fact, females have a greater likelihood (.465) of being adjudicated in the first 18 months after their first offense, whereas males have a greater likelihood (.364) of being adjudicated 19 to 36 months after their first offense. See Table B-5.1.

B-5.2   Delay and Race

Differential delay periods exist between black and white youths. Simply stated, blacks tend to remain in the community longer than whites after the first officially recorded offense. See Table B-5.2 and Figure B-5.2.

B-5.3   Delay and Level of Aggressiveness

Delay and the level of aggressiveness are statistically

dependent. In essence, the longer the period of delay in the community, the higher the probability of aggressive offense behavior. Similarly, nonaggressive offenses occur with the greatest frequency in the period of shortest delay. Figure B-5.3 demonstrates this definitive relationship quite well. Finally, chi-square analysis strongly supports this direct relationship between period of delay and the level of aggressiveness (ρ > .999). See Table B-5.3 and Figure B-5.3.

B-5.4   Delay and Age at First Offense

Delay and age of first offense are statistically dependent. In general, the younger the age at first offense, the longer the delay between that first offense and subsequent adjudication. Youth are generally entering the delinquency treatment system at approximately the same age, regardless of prior offense history. Those who commit their first offense at a young age experience longer delays and, as a result, are adjudicated at about the same age as those who commit their first offense at older ages and experience shorter delay periods. Chi-square analysis strongly supports this hypothesis of dependence between delay and age of first offense (ρ > .999). See Tables B-5.4.1 and B-5.4.2.

B-5.5   Delay and Age at Admission

In general, the older the youth at admission, the greater the probability that he has experienced a longer than average delay period. See Table B-5.5.

B-5.6   Summary: Delay

Two important facts have emerged from the discussion of delay. First, the average delay period is 21.6 months, although the period of delay varies considerably and should not be used as a definitive indicator. Second, longer delay periods are experienced primarily by black, male, and aggressive youth, whereas shorter delay periods are experienced by primarily by white, female, and nonaggressive youth.

TABLE B-1

SEX BY RACE

(Row and Column Percentages)

Sex	Race		Totals (N=410)
	White (N=171)	Black (N=239)	
Percent down:			
Male	76.0	75.7	75.9
Female	24.0	24.3	24.1
Totals	100.0	100.0	100.0
Percent across:			
Male (N=311)	41.8	58.2	100.0
Female (N=99)	41.4	58.6	100.0
Totals (N=410)	41.7	58.3	100.0

$\chi^2 = .0067$, df = 1, $.05 < \rho < .10$

TABLE B-2.1

OFFENSE CLASS BY SEX

(Row and Column Percentages)

Offense Class	Sex		Totals (N=416)
	Male (N=315)	Female (N=101)	
Percent down:			
Nonaggressive	32.7	85.1	45.4
Aggressive and noninjurious	31.1	5.0	24.8
Aggressive and injurious	36.2	10.9	29.8
Totals	100.0	100.0	100.0
Percent across:			
Nonaggressive (N=189)	54.5	45.5	100.0
Aggressive and non-injurious (N=103)	95.1	4.9	100.0
Aggressive and injurious (N=124)	91.9	8.1	100.0
Totals (N=416)	75.7	24.3	100.0

χ^2 - 85.16, df = 2, ρ > .999

TABLE B-2.2

OFFENSE CLASS BY RACE

(Row and Column Percentages)

Offense Class	Race		Totals (N=410)
	White (N=171)	Black (N=239)	
Percent down:			
Nonaggressive	56.7	36.8	45.4
Aggressive and noninjurious	25.7	23.8	24.5
Aggressive and injurious	17.6	39.4	40.1
Totals	100.0	100.0	100.0
Percent across:			
Nonaggressive (N=185)	52.4	47.6	100.0
Aggressive and non-injurious (N=101)	43.6	56.4	100.0
Aggressive and injurious (N=124)	24.2	75.8	100.0
Totals (N=410)	41.5	58.0	100.0

$\chi^2 = 27.0$, df = 2, $\rho > .999$

TABLE B-2.3

OFFENSE CLASS BY RACE AND SEX

(Row and Column Percentages)

Offense Level	White			Black			Totals (N=410)
	Male (N=130)	Female (N=41)	Totals (N=171)	Male (N=181)	Female (N=58)	Totals (N=239)	
Percent down:							
Nonaggressive	45.4	92.7	56.7	23.2	79.3	36.8	45.1
Aggressive and non-injurious	32.3	4.9	25.7	29.8	5.2	23.8	24.6
Aggressive and injurious	22.3	2.4	17.6	47.0	15.5	38.4	30.2
Totals	100.0	100.0	100.0	100.0	100.0	100.0	100.0
Percent across:							
Nonaggressive (N=185)	31.9	20.5	52.4	22.7	24.9	47.6	100.0
Aggressive and non-injurious (N=101)	41.6	1.9	43.5	53.5	3.0	56.5	100.0
Aggressive and injurious (N=124)	23.4	0.9	24.3	68.5	7.2	75.7	100.0
Totals (N=410)	31.7	10.0	41.7	44.2	14.1	58.3	100.0

x^2 = 149.34, df = 6, ρ > .999

104

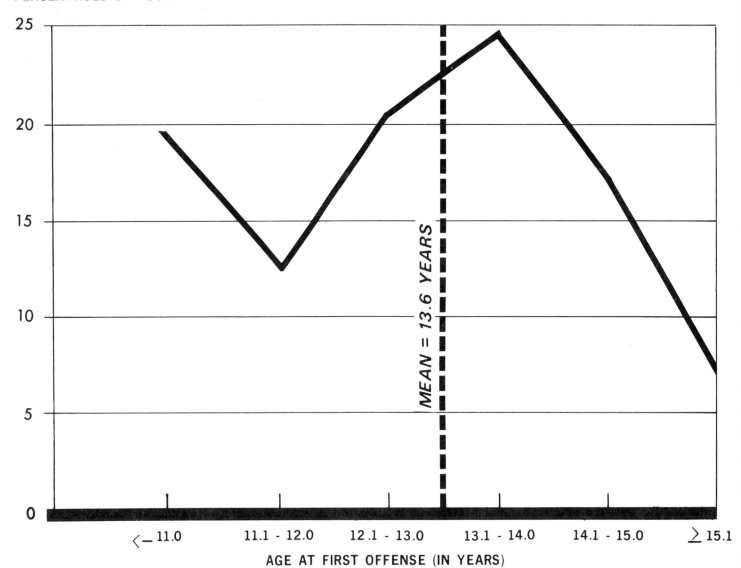

FIGURE B - 3

AGE AT FIRST OFFENSE

PERCENTAGES OF YOUTH

MEAN = 13.6 YEARS

AGE AT FIRST OFFENSE (IN YEARS)

TABLE B-3.1

AGE AT FIRST OFFENSE BY SEX

(Row and Column Percentages)

Age at First Offense	Sex		Totals (N=406)
	Male (N=307)	Female (N=99)	
Percent down:			
$\leq$ 12.0	33.2	24.2	31.0
12.1-14.0	41.4	54.6	44.6
$\geq$ 14.1	25.4	21.2	24.4
Totals	100.0	100.0	100.0
Percent across:			
$\leq$ 12.0 (N=126)	81.0	19.0	100.0
12.1-14.0 (N=181)	70.2	29.8	100.0
$\geq$ 14.1 (N=99)	78.8	21.2	100.0
Totals (N=406)	75.6	24.4	100.0

χ^2 = 5.39, df = 2, .90 < ρ < .95

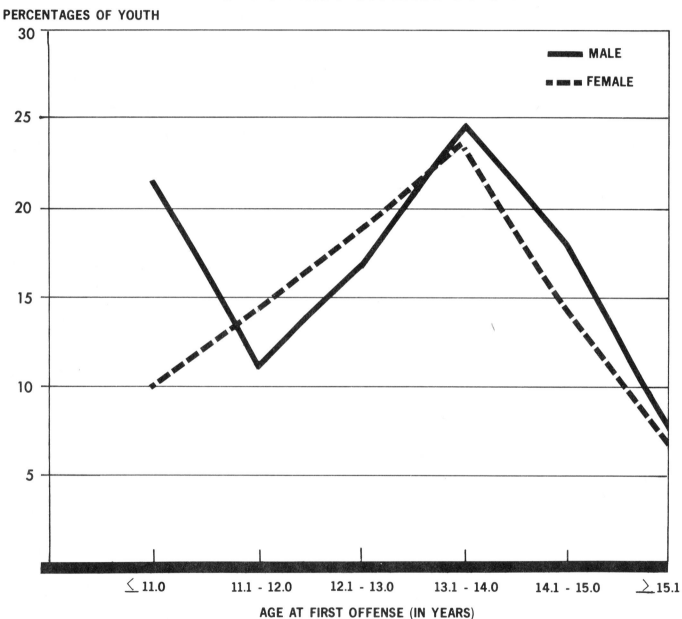

FIGURE B - 3.1

AGE AT FIRST OFFENSE BY SEX

PERCENTAGES OF YOUTH

MALE

FEMALE

AGE AT FIRST OFFENSE (IN YEARS)

TABLE B-3.2

AGE AT FIRST OFFENSE BY RACE

(Row and Column Percentages)

Age at First Offense	Race		Totals (N=410)
	White (N=166)	Black (N=235)	
Percent down:			
$\leq$ 12.0	26.5	34.0	30.8
12.1-14.0	45.8	44.3	44.9
$\geq$ 14.1	27.7	21.7	24.3
Totals	100.0	100.0	100.0
Percent across:			
$\leq$ 12.0 (N=124)	35.5	64.5	100.0
12.1-14.0 (N=180)	42.2	57.8	100.0
$\geq$ 14.1 (N=97)	46.9	52.1	100.0
Totals (N=401)	41.4	58.6	100.0

χ^2 = 3.29, df = 2, .80 < ρ < .90

TABLE B-3.3

AGE AT FIRST OFFENSE BY OFFENSE CLASS

(Row and Column Percentages)

Age at First Offense	Offense Class			Totals (N=406)
	Nonaggres- sive (N=181)	Aggressive and Noninjurious (N=103)	Aggressive and Injurious (N=122)	
Percent down:				
$\leq$ 12.0	22.7	34.9	40.2	31.0
12.1-14.0	53.0	37.9	37.7	44.6
$\geq$ 14.1	24.3	27.2	22.1	24.4
Totals	100.0	100.0	100.0	100.0
Percent across:				
$\leq$ 12.0 (N=126)	32.5	28.6	38.9	100.0
12.1-14.0 (N=181)	53.0	21.5	25.4	100.0
$\geq$ 14.1 (N=99)	44.4	28.3	27.3	100.0
Totals (N=406)	44.6	25.4	30.0	100.0

χ^2 = 13.7, df = 4, ρ > .999

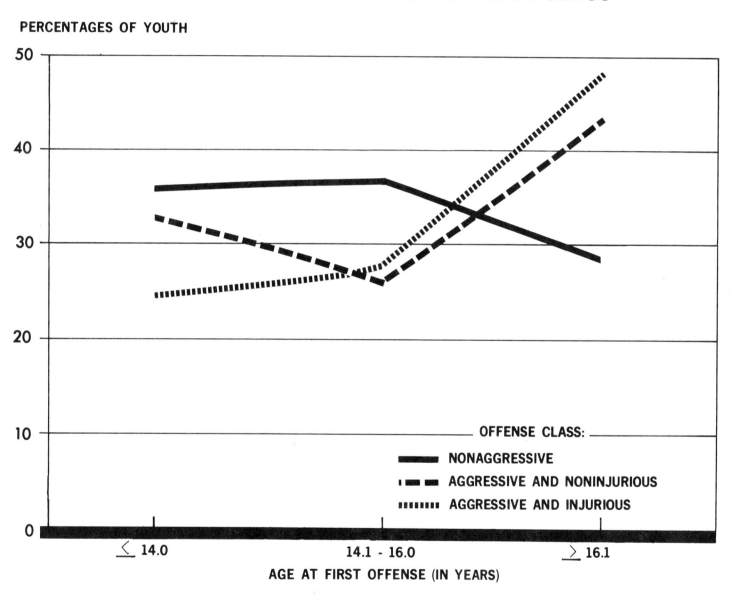

FIGURE B - 3.3

AGE AT FIRST OFFENSE BY OFFENSE CLASS

PERCENTAGES OF YOUTH

OFFENSE CLASS:

━━━━ NONAGGRESSIVE

▬ ▬ ▬ AGGRESSIVE AND NONINJURIOUS

▪▪▪▪▪▪▪ AGGRESSIVE AND INJURIOUS

AGE AT FIRST OFFENSE (IN YEARS)

110

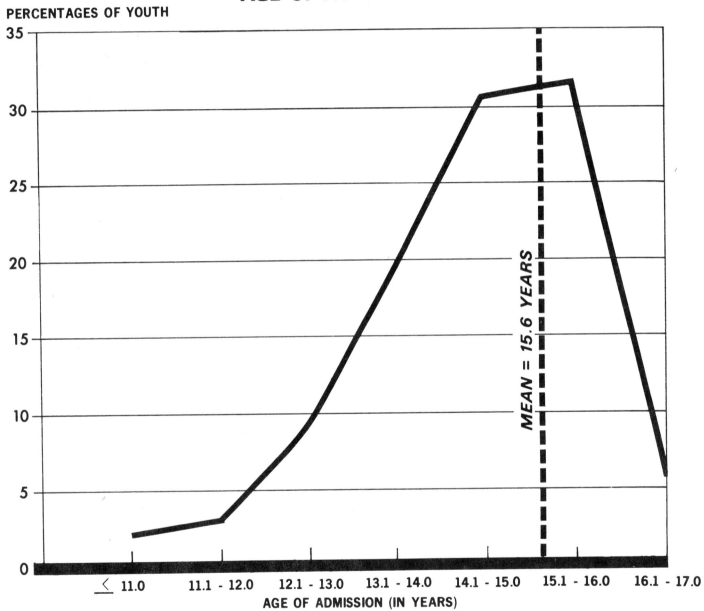

FIGURE B - 4

AGE OF ADMISSION

PERCENTAGES OF YOUTH

MEAN = 15.6 YEARS

AGE OF ADMISSION (IN YEARS)

TABLE B-4.1

AGE OF ADMISSION BY SEX

(Row and Column Percentages)

Age of Admission	Sex		Totals (N=415)
	Male (N=314)	Female (N=101)	
Percent down:			
$\leq$ 14.0	28.7	38.6	31.1
14.1-16.0	30.6	32.7	31.1
$\geq$ 16.1	30.6	28.7	37.8
Totals	100.0	100.0	100.0
Percent across:			
$\leq$ 14.0 (N=129)	69.8	30.2	100.0
14.1-16.0 (N=129)	74.4	25.6	100.0
$\geq$ 16.1 (N=57)	81.5	18.5	100.0
Totals (N=415)	75.7	24.3	100.0

χ^2 = 5.47, df = 2, .90 < ρ < .95

TABLE B-4.2

AGE OF ADMISSION BY RACE

(Row and Column Percentages)

Age of Admission	Race		Totals (N=409)
	White (N=171)	Black (N=238)	
Percent down:			
$\leq$ 14.0	32.2	31.1	31.4
14.1-16.0	31.6	30.2	30.9
$\geq$ 16.1	36.2	38.7	37.7
Totals	100.0	100.0	100.0
Percent across:			
$\leq$ 14.0 (N=129)	42.6	57.4	100.0
14.1-16.0 (N=126)	42.8	56.2	100.0
$\geq$ 16.1 (N=154)	40.0	59.7	100.0
Totals (N=409)	41.8	58.2	100.0

χ^2 = .24, df = 2, .50 < ρ < .70

TABLE B-4.3

AGE AT ADMISSION BY OFFENSE CLASS

(Row and Column Percentages)

Age at Admission	Offense Class			Totals (N=416)
	Nonaggressive (N=189)	Aggressive and Noninjurious (N=103)	Aggressive and Injurious (N=124)	
Percent down:				
≤ 14.1	35.0	32.0	25.0	31.3
14.1-16.0	35.9	26.2	27.4	31.0
≥ 16.1	29.1	41.8	47.6	37.7
Totals	100.0	100.0	100.0	100.0
Percent across:				
≤ 14.0 (N=130)	50.8	25.4	23.8	100.0
14.1-16.0 (N=129)	52.7	20.9	26.4	100.0
≥ 16.1 (N=157)	35.0	27.4	37.6	100.0
Totals (N=416)	45.4	24.8	29.8	100.0

$\chi^2 = 12.0$, df = 4, $.975 < \rho < .999$

FIGURE B - 4.3

AGE OF ADMISSION BY OFFENSE CLASS

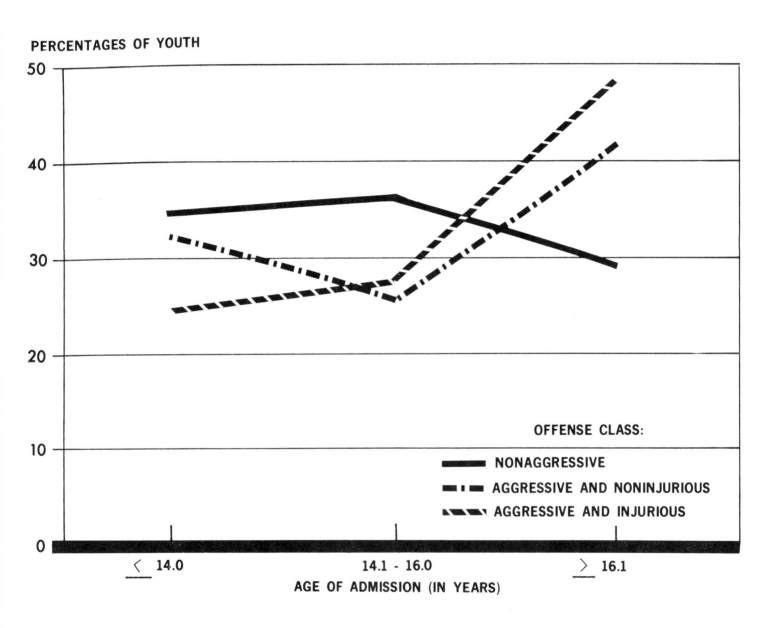

115

TABLE B-4.4

AGE OF ADMISSION BY AGE AT FIRST OFFENSE

(Row and Column Percentages)

Age at First Offense	Age at Admission			Totals (N=405)
	< 14.0 (N̄=126)	14.1-16.0 (N=124)	> 16.1 (N̄=155)	
Percent down:				
< 12.0	54.8	23.4	17.4	30.9
12.1-14.0	45.2	52.4	38.1	44.7
> 14.1	0.0	24.2	44.5	24.4
Totals	100.0	100.0	100.0	100.0
Percent across:				
< 12.0 (N=125)	55.2	23.2	21.6	100.0
12.1-16.0 (N=181)	31.5	35.9	32.6	100.0
> 16.1 (N=99)	0.0	30.3	69.7	100.0
Totals (N=405)	31.1	30.6	38.3	100.0

$\chi^2 = 94.17$, df = 4, p > .999

TABLE B-5.1

DELAY BY SEX

(Row and Column Percentages)

Delay	Sex		Totals (N=414)
	Male (N=313)	Female (N=101)	
Percent down:			
1-18 months	34.2	46.5	37.2
19-36 months	36.4	30.7	35.0
37-54 months	29.4	22.8	27.8
Totals	100.0	100.0	100.0
Percent across:			
1-18 months (N=154)	69.5	30.5	100.0
19-36 months (N=145)	78.6	21.4	100.0
37-54 months (N=115)	80.0	20.0	100.0
Totals (N=414)	75.6	24.4	100.0

$\chi^2 = 5.05$, df = 2, $.90 < \rho < .95$

TABLE B-5.2

DELAY BY RACE

(Row and Column Percentages)

Delay	Race		Totals (N=408)
	White (N=170)	Black (N=238)	
Percent down:			
1-18 months	42.4	33.6	37.3
19-36 months	34.7	35.7	35.4
37-54+ months	22.9	30.7	27.3
Totals	100.0	100.0	100.0
Percent across:			
1-18 months (N=151)	47.3	52.7	100.0
19-36 months (N=143)	41.0	59.0	100.0
37-54+ months (N=112)	34.8	65.2	100.0
Totals (N=408)	41.7	58.3	100.0

$\chi^2 = 4.73$, df = 2, $.90 < \rho < .95$

FIGURE B - 5.2

DELAY BY RACE

PERCENTAGES OF YOUTH

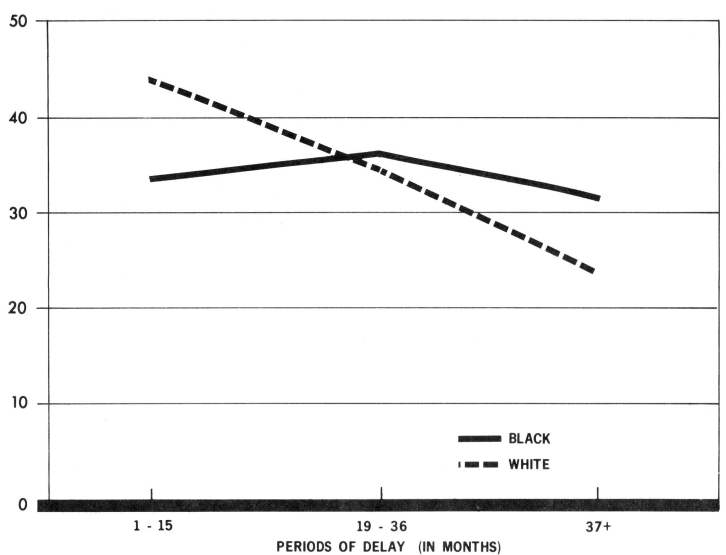

PERIODS OF DELAY (IN MONTHS)

TABLE B-5.3

DELAY BY OFFENSE CLASS

(Row and Column Percentages)

Delay	Offense Class			Totals (N=414)
	Nonaggressive (N=189)	Aggressive and Noninjurious (N=101)	Aggressive and Injurious (N=124)	
Percent down:				
1-18 months	47.1	32.7	25.8	37.2
19-37 months	34.4	37.6	33.9	35.0
38+ months	18.5	29.7	40.3	27.8
Totals	100.0	100.0	100.0	100.0
Percent across:				
1-18 months (N=154)	57.8	21.4	20.8	100.0
19-37 months (N=145)	44.8	26.2	29.0	100.0
38+ months (N=115)	30.4	26.1	43.5	100.0
Totals (N=414)	45.6	24.4	30.0	100.0

$\chi^2 = 65.09$, df = 4, $\rho > .999$

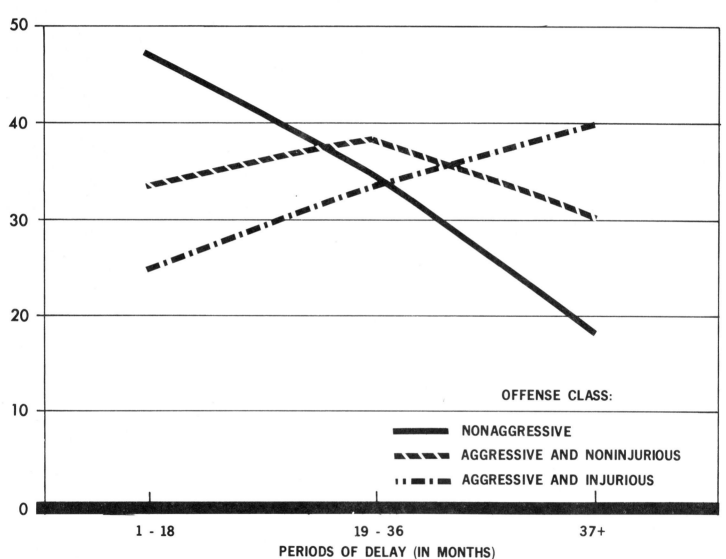

FIGURE B - 5.3

DELAY BY OFFENSE CLASS

PERCENTAGES OF YOUTH

TABLE B-5.4.1

DELAY BY AGE AT FIRST OFFENSE

(Row and Column Percentages)

Delay	Age at First Offense			Totals (N=404)
	$\leq$ 12.0 (N=154)	12.1-14.0 (N=145)	$\geq$ 14.1 (N=105)	
Percent down:				
1-18 months	5.6	39.8	77.3	38.1
19-36 months	27.0	49.2	22.7	35.9
37+ months	67.4	11.0	0.0	26.0
Totals	100.0	100.0	100.0	100.0
Percent across:				
1-18 months (N=126)	4.5	46.8	48.7	100.0
19-36 months (N=181)	23.4	61.4	15.2	100.0
37+ months (N=97)	80.1	19.9	0.0	100.0
Totals (N=404)	31.2	44.8	24.0	100.0

χ^2 = 214.75, df = 4, ρ > .999

TABLE B-5.4.2

DELAY BY OFFENSE CLASS AND AGE AT FIRST OFFENSE

(Row and Column Percentages)

Delay	Nonaggressive				Aggressive & Noninjurious				Aggressive & Injurious				Totals (N=384)
	<12.0 (N=23)	12.1-14.0 (N=70)	>14.1 (N=84)	Totals (N=177)	<12.0 (N=28)	12.1-14.0 (N=29)	>14.1 (N=38)	Totals (N=95)	<12.0 (N=36)	12.1-14.0 (N=36)	>14.1 (N=40)	Totals (N=112)	
Percent down:													
1-18 months	17.4	54.2	89.3	66.1	7.1	31.0	76.3	42.1	2.8	27.8	60.0	31.3	50.0
19-36 months	30.4	38.6	10.7	24.3	32.2	44.8	23.7	32.6	19.4	44.4	40.0	34.8	29.4
37+ months	52.2	7.2	0.0	9.6	60.7	24.2	0.0	25.3	77.8	27.8	0.0	33.9	20.6
Totals	100.0	100.0	100.0	100.0	100.0	100.0	100.0	100.0	100.0	100.0	100.0	100.0	100.0
Percent across:													
1-18 months (N=192)	2.1	19.8	39.1	61.0	1.0	4.7	15.1	20.8	0.5	5.2	12.5	18.2	100.0
19-36 months (N=113)	6.2	23.9	8.0	38.1	8.0	11.5	8.0	27.5	6.2	14.1	14.1	34.4	100.0
37+ months (N=79)	15.2	6.3	0.0	21.5	21.5	8.9	0.0	30.4	35.4	12.7	0.0	48.1	100.0
Totals	6.0	18.2	21.9	46.1	7.3	7.5	9.9	24.7	9.4	9.4	10.4	29.2	100.0

$x^2 = 220.28$, df = 16, $p > .999$

TABLE B-5.5

DELAY BY AGE OF ADMISSION

(Row and Column Percentages)

Delay	Age at Admission			Totals (N=413)
	$\leq$ 14.0 (N=121)	14.1-16.0 (N=128)	$\geq$ 16.1 (N=156)	
Percent down:				
1-18 months	40.3	43.7	29.5	37.3
19-36 months	34.1	30.5	39.7	35.1
37+ months	25.6	25.8	30.8	27.6
Totals	100.0	100.0	100.0	100.0
Percent across:				
1-18 months (N=154)	33.8	36.4	29.8	100.0
19-36 months (N=145)	30.3	26.9	42.8	100.0
37+ months (N=114)	28.9	28.9	42.2	100.0
Totals (N=413)	31.2	31.0	37.8	100.0

χ^2 = 6.91, df = 4, .80 < ρ < .90

APPENDIX C
ADDENDUM TO CHAPTER 4

This appendix includes a more detailed description of the variables
affecting the intake and placement-
making processes. The tables included
in this appendix correspond section-
by-section with the narrative of the
appendix.

Also included in this appendix is a
description of the Youth Opinion Poll
referred to on page 27. This section
of the appendix is labeled C-4 and
begins on page 137.

C-1   Intake

Section 4.3 of Chapter 4 addresses one main question: Are youth who take part in the intake process being differentially selected for the various intake modalities? The answer to this question can be discerned by examining the basic demographic characteristics of the direct court, directly placed, and Intake Center placed subpopulations and determining if any differences exist between them.

C-1.1   Intake and Sex

The data strongly suggests that intake participation is, in part, a function of the sex of the youth. Specifically, 35 percent of the male population participates in the Intake Center process, compared to only 21 percent of the female population. On the other hand, 14 percent of the female, as opposed to 10 percent of the male population is placed by the Wayne County Court. Sixty-two percent of the female and 56 percent of the male population are in the direct intake group. See Table C-1.1. Chi-square analysis supports this hypothesis of dependence $(.95 < \rho < .975)$.

C-1.2   Intake and Race

A significant interaction exists between intake process participation and race. In essence, this significance is a result of a greater within-race proportion of Intake Center placements for blacks than for whites, whereas there is a greater within-race proportion of Wayne County Court placements for whites than for blacks. Specifically, 35 percent of the black population were placed by the Intake Center, compared to 26 percent of the white population; 20 percent of the white and only 4 percent of the black population were placed by the Wayne County Court. Chi-square analysis supports this significant interaction $(\rho > .995)$.

By excluding the youth placed by the Wayne County Court, the dependence between race and intake is eliminated $(\rho = .50)$. Hence, the significant interaction between race and intake is to a large degree a result of a greater than expected frequency of white youth placement by the Wayne County Court, and not directly related to Department of

Social Services intake functions.   See tables C-1.2.1 and C-1.2.2.

C-1.3   Intake and the Level of Aggressiveness

The data strongly suggests the existence of a significant dependence between the level of aggressiveness and the intake process. Sixty-five percent of all Intake Center youth had committed aggressive offenses prior to adjudication. Only 54 percent of the direct and 29 percent of the Wayne County Court placed youth were aggressive. On the other hand, 46 percent of the directly placed and 72 percent of the Wayne County Court placed youth were nonaggressive. Hence, Intake Center youth can be considered to be more aggressive than direct and Wayne County Court youth. Chi-square analysis supports this dependence between intake and the target of aggressiveness when the County Court is included ($\rho > .999$) or excluded ($\rho > .99$). See Table C-1.3.

C-1.4   Intake and Age at First Offense

With the inclusion of the Wayne County Court subpopulation, there is a significant dependence between intake and age at first offense ($\rho > .95$). However, when the Wayne County Court subpopulation is removed from the analysis, the dependence between intake and first offense is eliminated ($\rho = .10$). The significant dependence created by the Wayne County Court subpopulation is due to the court's placement of a predominance of youth between twelve and fourteen years of age. In fact, 66 percent of this subpopulation is in the 12.1-14.0 age range, which is 1.5 times the expected frequency for that group. On the other hand, actual frequencies for all age groups placed directly or by the Intake Center do not deviate significantly from expected frequencies. Hence, when examining only the subpopulations served by the Department of Social Services, age at first offense has apparently not been used as a criteria for intake process selection. See Table C-1.4.

C-1.5   Intake and Age at Admission

The data suggests that the relationship between the age at admission and intake is independent. The relationship holds when the Wayne County Court subpopulation is included ($.30 < \rho < .50$) or excluded ($.50 < \rho < .70$). All within and between group actual frequencies are approximately equal to their expected values. Therefore, age of admission is not a criteria for intake process selection. See Table C-1.5.

C-1.6   Intake and Delay

The data suggests that the interaction between intake and delay is not sigificant. This is true for both the inclusion $(.30 < \rho < .50)$ and exclusion $(.30 < \rho < .50)$ of the Wayne County Court subpopulation. Hence, delay does not appear to be a significant factor in intake process selection procedures. See Table C-1.6.

C-1.7   Summary: Intake

The intake demographics section has addressed one central question: What types of youth are selected for the three different intake processes? The answer to this question comes from the salient points listed below that have emerged from the above discussion.

First, males received a greater within group proportion of intake center placements than did females, whereas females received a greater within group proportion of direct and Wayne County Court populations. Second, race is a significant characteristic when considering all three processes, for the Wayne County Court accepts mainly white youth. When viewing only the intake and direct subpopulations, race is not a significant selection criteria. Third, Intake Center populations are somewhat more aggressive than the direct subpopulation and predominantly more aggressive than the Wayne County Court's subpopulation. Youth who commit their first offense at earlier ages are placed more frequently by the Wayne County Court than by the Intake Center or the intake staff located in the Youth Home. There is no statistical difference between the intake and direct subpopulations for age at first offense.

C-2   Intake and Initial Placement

One of the most crucial aspects in the analysis of the Intake Center process is the pattern of placements that result from this process. Hence this section will attempt to discern whether or not youth are being differentially placed by the Intake Center.

Chi-square analysis indicates that the interaction between intake and initial placement is highly significant. Furthermore, this relationship remains valid whether or not the Wayne County Court subpopulation remains in the analysis ($\rho > .999$) or is excluded ($\rho > .999$).

Specifically, 47 percent of the Intake Center population is placed in either public or private institutions, whereas 81 percent of the directly placed youth and 93 percent of the Wayne County Court youth are institutionalized. Similarly, 19 percent of the Intake Center youth receive community nonresidential care placements, only five percent of the directly placed youth and none of the Wayne County Court youth received this type of placement. Finally, 35 percent of the Intake Center youth were placed in community residential care facilities, compared to 14 and seven percent for the directly placed and Wayne County Court youth, respectively.

In sum, youth are, on the basis of initial placement alone, receiving differential placement as a function of intake process involvement. See Table C-2.

C-2.1   Intake, Initial Placement and Sex

Within the Intake Center population, males received approximately the same frequency of institutional placements, 50 percent, as did females. However, within the direct intake population, males were institutionalized at a frequency of 86 percent, compared to females who were institutionalized at a frequency of 70 percent. All Wayne County Court males were institutionalized, as were 79 percent of the females.

Intake Center males were placed in community nonresidential placements at a frequency of 26 percent, whereas Intake Center females were placed in the same type of facility only 10 percent of the time. Both male and female direct intake youth were placed in the non-residential care facilities at a five percent frequency. Again, no Wayne County Court youth received nonresidential care placements.

Females were placed in community residential care facilities at a much greater frequency than males within all intake functions.

for the Intake Center population, females were placed in these facilities at a frequency of 38 percent, compared to the Intake Center male frequency of 26 percent. Twenty-five percent of the direct intake females received community residential care placements, compared to nine percent of the males. Twenty-one percent of the Wayne County Court females and none of the males were placed in those facilities.

Indeed, it is most fair to conclude that youth are being placed differentially by sex within and between the various intake processes. See Table C-2.1.

C-2.2   Intake, Initial Placement and Race

In evaluating the interaction of intake, initial placement and race, it is found that a significant dependence does exist between these variables. The significance is due, in the main, to the deviation from expected values for racial composition within the various intake processes, and to the subsequent placements made by the differential intake process.

Placement frequencies for white and black Intake Center youths are essentially equal, except for community residential care placements where whites received a seven percent greater placement frequency. For direct intake youth, 88 percent of the white youth were institutionalized, compared to 78 percent of the black youth. Moreover, 18 percent of the black youth were placed in community residential care facilities, as opposed to only eight percent of the white youth. Finally, only seven percent of the Wayne County youth were not placed in institutions. Hence, there is a basic racial element in the initial placement of the youth, due primarily to the differential intake process. See Table C-2.2.

C-2.3   Intake, Initial Placement and Level of Aggressiveness

There is a significant dependence between initial placement, intake process and offense level of aggressiveness ($p > .999$). This significance is due not only to the interaction of intake process and initial placement, but to the youth's offense behavior before adjudication as well.

For Intake Center youth, the aggressive and noninjurious offender was institutionalized 60 percent of the time, which was greater than the institutional frequency of 40 percent for both nonaggressive and aggressive and injurious youth. The inverse to this institutional placement pattern exists for community residential care placements. Nonaggressive youth were placed in this type of facility at a rate of 37 percent, aggressive and injurious at a rate of 32 percent and aggressive and noninjurious youth at a rate of 17 percent. For community nonresidential facilities, utilization was approximately the same for all offense levels, ranging from 22 percent for nonaggressive youth to 26 percent for aggressive and injurious youth. As would be expected, nonaggressive youth were placed most frequently in the community. In summary, the significant aspect for Intake Center youth is that aggressive and injurious youth received a much lower proportion of institutional placements than did aggressive and noninjurious youth. Concomitantly, these aggressive and injurious one youth received a much greater proportion of community placements than did the supposed less serious offender, the aggressive noninjurious youth.

Directly placed youth exhibited a somewhat different placement trend compared to Intake Center youth. Nonaggressive youth were placed in the institutions 77 percent of the time, whereas aggressive youth, both injurious and noninjurious, were institutionalized at a rate of about 86 percent. Furthermore, both nonaggressive and aggressive noninjurious youth were placed in community residential care facilities about 15 percent of the time, compared to the aggressive and injurious youth rate of nine percent. Finally, community nonresidential care placements were utilized only minimally, with aggressive injurious and nonaggressive youth being placed at a rate of about five percent. No aggressive noninjurious youth received this type of placement. There is, then, a small degree of differential placement relative to prior offense behavior occurring in the direct placement function, i.e., more aggressive than nonaggressive youth are being institutionalized.

However, it must be stressed that the great majority of all directly placed youth, 81 percent, are placed in institutions.

The Wayne County Court exhibits essentially no planned differential placement. Ninety-three percent of these youth are placed in institutions regardless of offense level. The remaining seven percent of the youth were placed in community residential care facilities. The absence of differentiation is even more apparent when one considers the fact that more than 70 percent of these youth were nonaggressive, of whom over 90 percent were institutionalized. See Table C-2.3.

In sum, the data strongly suggests that the Intake Center is differentially placing youth according to their prior offense history, with nonaggressive and aggressive and injurious youth receiving a significantly larger proportion of community placements than did aggressive and injurious youth. Some differential placement does exist for directly placed youth, but the predominance of their placements are to institutions. Finally, the Wayne County Court institutionalizes all but a very small proportion of their youth.

C-2.4   Intake, Initial Placement, and Age at First Offense

The data indicates that age at first offense does have an effect upon placement decisions made by staff located at the Intake Center and intake staff at the Youth Home. In general, the younger a youth's age at first offense, the more likely the youth is to receive an institutional placement. Conversely, the older the youth's age at first offense, the more likely the youth will receive a community placement. These relationships hold for both Intake Center and directly placed youth. The magnitude of placement frequency differences between age groups is not large enough to be indicative of a regularly used criteria. However, the consistent pattern within both Intake Center and direct placement processes necessitates its mention. This pattern does not exist for Wayne County Court youth, for almost all of these youth regardless of age at first offense, were institutionalized.

C-2.5   Intake, Initial Placement, and Age of Admission

For the interaction of initial placement, intake and age of admission, no significant dependence was found beyond the degree contributed by initial placement and intake.

C-2.6   Intake, Initial Placement and Delay

As was the case above, delay made no significant contribution to the degree of dependency between initial placement and intake.

C-2.7   Summary: Intake and Initial Placement

In general, a strong pattern of differential placement exists for youth placed out of the Intake Center. The significant aspects of this pattern are:

1. Males have a higher likelihood of community nonresidential placement than do females, at the same time, females have a higher likelihood of community residential placement than do males.

2. Aggressive noninjurious youth have a greater probability of being institutionalized than do nonaggressive or aggressive injurious youth, whereas nonaggressive and aggressive injurious youth have a greater probability of community placement than do aggressive noninjurious youth.

3. The younger the youth is at age at first offense, the greater the likelihood he or she will receive an institutional placement. Conversely, the older the youth is at age at first offense, the greater the likelihood he or she will receive a community placement.

Furthermore, for directly placed youth, a placement pattern does exist but is much less apparent. These patterns are:

1. Males have a greater likelihood of institutional placement than females, although the likelihood of institutionalization is quite high (.81) for both sexes.

134

2. Aggressive youth have a larger probability of being placed in institutions than do nonaggressive youth.

3. As was demonstrated for Intake Center youth the younger a youth is at age at first offense, the higher the probability of the youth's institutionalization, whereas the older the youth at age at first offense, the higher the probability of the youth's community placement.

Finally, for Wayne County Court youth, emphasis is upon placing the nonaggressive youth in private institutions. For males and females, 93 percent were institutionalized.

C-3   Initial Placement

Initial placement will be used to determine the distribution of the state ward population by demographic characteristics across the various placement facilities.

C-3.1   Initial Placement and Sex

There is a strong indication that initial placement and sex are dependent. Greater than expected frequencies are observed for males placed in institutions and community nonresidential care facilities, and females placed in community residential care facilities. Seventy-three percent of all males are institutionalized compared to 65 percent of all females. Moreover, 11 percent of all males are placed in community nonresidential care facilities, while only two percent of the females receive this type of placement. Finally, 33 percent of the female population receive community residential care placements, contrasted with only 16 percent of the male population. Therefore, the sex of any particular youth has probably been a determining factor in the placement of that youth. See Table C-3.1.

C-3.2   Initial Placement and Race

The data indicates that race is also a determining factor in the initial placement decision. Specifically, white youth were institutionalized 79 percent of the time compared to blacks who were institutionalized 65 percent of the time. Furthermore, 25 percent of all blacks were placed in community residential care facilities, versus only 15 percent of the white population. Actual frequencies for white and black youth are approximately equal to their expected values for all community nonresidential placements. In essence, race is somewhat indicative of initial placement as whites receive more institutional placements, while blacks are placed at a greater frequency in community residential care facilities.

The interaction between initial placement, sex and race generates additional significant findings. White females are placed in institutions at an 80 percent frequency compared to only a 55 percent frequency for black females. Furthermore, 38 percent of the black females were placed in community residential care facilities, compared to only 17 percent of the white females. See Table C-3.2.

C-3.3   Initial Placement and Level of Aggressiveness

The interaction between initial placement and level of aggressiveness is not significant (.80 < ρ < .90). However, nonaggressive youth were placed in the institutions less frequently and in community residential care facilities more frequently than both types of aggressive youth. Paradoxically, aggressive youth received more community nonresidential care placements (32 percent) than did the nonaggressive youth (25 percent). See Tables C-3.3.1 and C-3.3.2.

C-3.4   Initial Placement and Age at First Offense

Initial placement and age at first offense are statistically independent attributes (.80 < ρ < .90). The actual frequencies for initial placement within each age of first offense group are approximately equal to their expected frequencies for all possible available combinations. See Table C-3.4.

C-3.5   Initial Placement and Age at Admission

Initial placement and age at admission are also statistically independent attributes (.50 < ρ < .70). All deviation of actual frequency from expected frequency is random in nature, hence the insignificant chi-square value. See Table C-3.5.

C-3.6   Initial Placement and Delay

Consistent with age at first offense and age at admission, initial placement and delay are statistically independent attributes $(.80 < \rho < .90)$. See Table C-3.6.1.

C-3.7   Summary: Initial Placement

Only two attributes, sex and race, were found to yield a significant dependence with initial placement. In the main, however, this effect is due to placement differences between black and white females. White females are institutionalized at a greater frequency than black females, whereas black females receive a greater proportion of community residential placements than do white females.

C-4   Youth Opinion Poll Scales

The Youth Opinion Poll is a 240 item true-false questionnaire designed to measure youths' attitudes. It is administered to a youth on a pre and post test basis. That is, each youth is given the questionnaire when he enters a placement and again when he leaves the same placement. The Youth Opinion Poll measures the youth's attitude change during the placement period. The questionnaire measures attitudes on ten scales. They are described below.

C-4.1   Infrequency Scale (17 items)

This scale serves to check for random responding by the youth. It is comprised of questions which should be answered the same by all youth if they are listening. Sample questions include, "I've never seen an apple" and "I cannot believe that wood really burns." If six or more of these questions are answered incorrectly the questionnaire is considered invalid and it is given again the next day.

C-4.2   Social Desirability Scale[1] (20 items)

This scale is intended to detect a "fake good" response. That is, subjects may either consciously or unconsciously be responding to the desirability of the item rather than to the item content. A high score on this scale may indicate image management, typically high self regard, or a high degree of conventional socialization. Sample questions from this scale are, "I always try to be considerate of my friends" and "I am not willing to give up my own privacy or pleasure in order to help other people."

C-4.3   Nurturance Scale[2] (20 items)

The Nurturance Scale measures a youth's attitudes towards others. Items on this scale refer to attitudes towards infants, helping others, and caring for the sick. Sample questions from this scale

---

[1]Personality Research Form

[2]Personality Research Form

138

are, "I really do not pay much attention to people when they talk about their problems" and "I believe in giving friends lots of help and advice."

C-4.4   Locus of Responsibility and Control Scale[3] (20 items)

This scale discriminates between an orientation of "things happen to me" and "I make things happen to me." Many delinquents do not accept responsibility for the consequences of their own acts. A high score on this scale would indicate that a youth feels he has control over his own life events. Sample questions from this scale are, "When you do good on a test at school it's probably because you studied for it" and "A person's worth often goes unnoticed no matter how hard he tries."

C-4.5   Critical Indicators of Positive Peer Culture (6 items plus 88 items overlapping in the other scales)

Positive Peer Culture is designed to teach certain attitudes therefore, if the program is reaching its goals, youth should score high on these items. This scale would allow comparison between PPC and non-PPC treatment modalities. Sample questions from the scale are, "I don't think it is necessary to step on others in order to get ahead in the world" and "I want to remain unbothered by obligations to friends."

C-4-6   Self-Esteem Scale[4] (57 items)

Low self-esteem is considered one of the characteristics of delinquents and it can become a self-fulfilling prophesy. The higher a youth scores on this scale the higher his self-esteem and the better he feels about himself. Sample questions include, "I often get discouraged in school" and "I'm popular with kids my own age."

---

[3]Rotter's Locus of Control Scale: Adapted

[4]Coopersmiths Self-Esteem Inventory

QUAY SCALES[5] (3 Scales)

C-4.7   Quay I: Psychopathic Delinquency (45 items)

This scale reflects tough, amoral, rebellious qualities coupled with impulsiveness, distrust of authority and freedom from family or other interpersonal ties. The higher a youth scores on this scale the more attitudes he holds that are classified as psychopathic/unsocialized. Sample questions from the scale are, "It's alright to steal from the rich because they don't need it" and "The worst thing a person can do is get caught."

C-4.8   Quay II: Neurotic Delinquency (30 items)

This scale measures impulsive and aggressive tendencies accompanied by tension, guilt, remorse, depression, and discouragement. A high score on this scale would indicate a neurotic-disturbed youth according to the Quay System. Sample questions from this scale include, "I think people like me as much as they do other people," and "I sometimes feel that no one loves me."

C-4.9   Quay III: Subcultural Delinquency (25 items)

This scale reflects attitudes, values, and behaviors commonly thought to occur among members of culturally and economically disadvantaged delinquent gangs. A high score on this scale would indicate a youth holds attitudes classified as sub-cultural-socialized by the Quay System. Sample questions from the scale are, "I would be a happier person if I could satisfy all my parents' wishes" and "I have never been in trouble with the law."

C-4.10   Total Quay Score

The PPC evaluation considers the total score of the three Quay Scales to determine an over-all delinquency orientation.

---

[5]Quays Personal Opinion Study

140

TABLE C-1.1

INTAKE PROCESS BY SEX

(Row and Column Percentages)

Intake Process	Sex		Totals (N=413)
	Male (N=315)	Female (N=98)	
Percent down:			
Intake	34.9	20.8	31.7
Direct	55.6	62.4	57.6
Wayne County	9.5	13.8	10.7
Totals	100.0	100.0	100.0
Percent across:			
Intake (N=131)	84.0	16.0	100.0
Direct (N=238)	73.5	26.5	100.0
Wayne County (N=44)	68.2	31.8	100.0
Totals (N=413)	76.3	23.7	100.0

$\chi^2 = 6.82$, df = 2, $.95 < \rho < .975$

TABLE C-1.2.1

INTAKE PROCESS BY RACE

(Row and Column Percentages)

Intake Process	Race		Totals (N=407)
	White (N=170)	Black (N=237)	
Percent down:			
Intake	26.5	35.5	31.5
Direct	53.5	60.3	57.7
Wayne County	20.0	4.2	10.8
Totals	100.0	100.0	100.0
Percent across:			
Intake (N=129)	34.9	65.1	100.0
Direct (N=234)	38.8	61.2	100.0
Wayne County (N=44)	77.3	22.7	100.0
Totals (N=407)	41.8	58.2	100.0

χ^2 = 26.28, df = 2, ρ > .995 (Including Wayne County Court)

χ^2 = 3.23, df = 2, .90 < ρ < .95 (Excluding Wayne County Court)

TABLE C-1.2.2

INTAKE PROCESS BY RACE AND SEX

(Row and Column Percentages)

INTAKE PROCESS	WHITE			BLACK			TOTALS (N=407)
	Male (N=130)	Female (N=40)	Totals (N=170)	Male (N=181)	Female (N=56)	Totals (N=237)	
Percent down:							
Intake	30.8	12.5	26.5	38.1	26.8	35.1	31.7
Direct	50.7	62.5	53.5	58.6	66.1	59.8	57.5
Wayne County Court	18.5	25.0	20.0	3.3	7.1	4.1	10.8
Totals	100.0	100.0	100.0	100.0	100.0	100.0	100.0
Percent across:							
Intake (N=129)	31.0	3.9	34.9	53.5	11.6	65.1	100.0
Direct (N=234)	28.2	10.7	38.9	45.3	15.8	61.1	100.0
Wayne County Court (N=44)	54.5	22.7	77.2	13.7	9.1	22.8	100.0
Totals (N=407)	31.9	9.8	41.7	44.5	13.8	58.3	100.0

$X^2 = 34.25$, df = 6, $\rho > .999$

TABLE C-1.3

INTAKE PROCESS BY OFFENSE CLASS

(Row and Column Percentages)

Intake Process	Offense Class			Totals (N=413)
	Nonaggressive (N=187)	Aggressive and Noninjurious (N=103)	Aggressive and Injurious (N=123)	
Percent down:				
Intake	24.6	45.6	30.9	31.7
Direct	58.3	50.5	62.6	57.6
Court	17.1	3.9	6.5	10.7
Totals	100.0	100.0	100.0	100.0
Percent across:				
Intake (N=131)	35.1	35.9	29.0	100.0
Direct (N=238)	45.8	21.8	32.4	100.0
Court (N=44)	72.4	9.1	18.2	100.0
Totals (N=413)	45.3	24.9	29.8	100.0

$\chi^2 = 24.56$, df = 4, $\rho > .999$

TABLE C-1.4

INTAKE PROCESS BY AGE AT FIRST OFFENSE

(Row and Column Percentages)

Intake Process	Age at First Offense			Totals (N=403)
	$\leq$ 12.0 (N=124)	12.1-14.0 (N=181)	$\geq$ 14.1 (N=98)	
Percent down:				
Intake	31.5	29.8	30.6	30.5
Direct	62.9	54.1	61.2	58.6
Wayne County	5.6	16.1	8.2	10.9
Totals	100.0	100.0	100.0	100.0
Percent across:				
Intake (N=123)	31.7	43.9	24.4	100.0
Direct (N=236)	33.1	41.5	25.4	100.0
Wayne County (N=44)	15.9	65.9	18.2	100.0
Totals (N=403)	30.8	44.9	24.3	100.0

χ^2 = 9.3, df = 4, ρ > .95 (Including Wayne County Court)

χ^2 = .177, df = 2, .05 < ρ < .10 (Excluding Wayne County Court)

TABLE C-1.5

INTAKE PROCESS BY AGE OF ADMISSION

(Row and Column Percentages)

Intake Process	Age of Admission			Totals (N=412)
	$\leq$ 14.0 ($\overline{N}$=129)	14.1-16.0 (N=127)	$\geq$ 16.1 ($\overline{N}$=156)	
Percent down:				
Intake	31.0	34.7	30.1	31.8
Direct	55.8	53.5	62.2	57.8
Wayne County	13.2	11.8	7.7	10.7
Totals	100.0	100.0	100.0	100.0
Percent across:				
Intake (N=131)	30.5	33.6	35.9	100.0
Direct (N=237)	30.4	28.7	40.9	100.0
Wayne County (N=44)	38.6	34.1	27.3	100.0
Totals (N=412)	31.3	30.9	37.8	100.0

χ^2 = 3.7, df = 4, .50 < ρ < .30

TABLE C-1.6

INTAKE PROCESS AND DELAY

(Row and Column Percentages)

Intake Process	Delay			Totals (N=408)
	1-18 months (N=207)	19-36 months (N=112)	37+ months (N=89)	
Percent down:				
Intake	30.0	31.3	36.0	31.6
Direct	57.5	58.0	58.4	57.8
Wayne County	12.5	10.7	5.6	10.6
Totals	100.0	100.0	100.0	100.0
Percent across:				
Intake (N=129)	48.1	27.1	24.8	100.0
Direct (N=236)	50.4	27.5	22.1	100.0
Wayne County (N=43)	60.5	27.9	11.6	100.0
Totals (N=408)	50.8	27.4	21.8	100.0

χ^2 = 3.6, df = 4, .50 < ρ < .70

TABLE C-2

INTAKE PROCESS BY INITIAL PLACEMENT

(Row and Column Percentages)

Intake Process	Initial Placement			Totals (N=413)
	Insti- tution (N=295)	Community Non- Residential Care (N=37)	Community Residential Care (N=81)	
Percent down:				
Intake	20.7	67.6	55.6	31.7
Direct	65.4	32.4	40.7	57.6
Wayne County	13.9	0.0	3.7	10.7
Totals	100.0	100.0	100.0	100.0
Percent across:				
Intake (N=131)	46.6	19.1	35.3	100.0
Direct (N=238)	81.1	5.0	13.9	100.0
Wayne County (N=44)	93.2	0.0	6.8	100.0
Totals (N=413)	71.4	9.0	19.6	100.0

χ^2 = 60.24, df = 4, ρ > .999 (Including Wayne County Court)

χ^2 = 49.52, df = 2, ρ > .999 (Excluding Wayne County Court)

TABLE C-2.1

INITIAL PLACEMENT BY INTAKE PROCESS AND SEX

(Row and Column Percentages)

Initial Placement	Intake Center			Direct Intake			Wayne County Court			Totals (N=413)
	Male (N=110)	Female (N=21)	Total (N=131)	Male (N=175)	Female (N=63)	Total (N=238)	Male (N=30)	Female (N=14)	Total (N=44)	
Percent down:										
Institutions	47.2	52.4	48.1	86.3	69.8	81.9	100.0	78.6	93.2	72.4
Community nonresidential	26.4	9.5	23.7	4.6	4.8	4.6	0.0	0.0	0.0	10.2
Community residential	26.4	38.1	28.2	9.1	25.4	13.5	0.0	21.4	6.8	17.4
Total	100.0	100.0	100.0	100.0	100.0	100.0	100.0	100.0	100.0	100.0
Percent across:										
Institutions (N=299)	17.4	3.7	21.1	50.5	14.7	65.2	10.0	3.7	13.7	100.0
Community nonresidential (N=42)	69.0	4.8	73.8	19.1	7.1	26.2	0.0	0.0	0.0	100.0
Community residential (N=72)	40.3	11.1	51.4	22.2	22.2	44.4	0.0	4.2	4.2	100.0
Total (N=413)	26.6	5.1	31.7	42.4	15.2	57.6	7.3	3.4	10.7	100.0

$\chi^2 = 83.22$, df = 16, $\rho > .999$

TABLE C-2.2

INITIAL PLACEMENT BY INTAKE PROCESS AND RACE

(Row and Column Percentages)

Initial Placement	Intake			Non-Intake			Wayne County Court			Total (N=407)
	White (N=45)	Black (N=84)	Total (N=129)	White (N=91)	Black (N=143)	Total (N=234)	White (N=34)	Black (N=10)	Total (N=44)	
Percent down:										
Institutions	44.5	48.8	47.3	87.9	78.3	82.0	97.1	80.0	93.2	72.2
Community nonresidential	22.2	25.0	24.0	4.4	4.2	4.3	0.0	0.0	0.0	10.1
Community residential	33.3	26.2	28.7	7.7	17.5	13.7	2.9	20.0	6.8	17.7
Total	100.0	100.0	100.0	100.0	100.0	100.0	100.0	100.0	100.0	100.0
Percent across:										
Institutions (N=274)	6.8	13.9	20.7	27.2	38.1	65.3	11.2	2.7	13.9	100.0
Community nonresidential (N=41)	24.4	51.2	75.6	9.8	14.6	24.4	0.0	0.0	0.0	100.0
Community residential (N=72)	20.8	30.6	51.4	9.7	34.7	44.4	1.4	2.8	4.2	100.0
Total (N=407)	11.1	20.6	31.7	22.4	35.1	57.5	8.3	2.5	10.8	100.0

$\chi^2 = 74.19$, df = 16, $\rho > .999$

TABLE C-2.3

INITIAL PLACEMENT BY INTAKE PROCESS AND OFFENSE CLASS

(Row and Column Percentages)

Initial Placement	Intake				Non-Intake				Wayne County Court				Total (N=413)
	Non-aggressive (N=46)	Aggressive & non-injurious (N=47)	Aggressive & injurious (N=38)	Total (N=131)	Non-aggressive (N=109)	Aggressive & non-injurious (N=52)	Aggressive & injurious (N=77)	Total (N=238)	Non-aggressive (N=32)	Aggressive & non-injurious (N=4)	Aggressive & injurious (N=8)	Total (N=44)	
Percent down:													
Institutions	41.3	59.6	42.1	46.6	77.1	86.5	85.7	81.1	90.6	100.0	100.0	93.2	72.4
Community nonresidential	21.7	23.4	26.3	19.1	6.4	0.0	5.2	4.6	0.0	0.0	0.0	0.0	10.2
Community residential	37.0	17.0	31.6	35.3	16.5	13.5	9.1	13.5	9.4	0.0	0.0	6.8	17.4
Total	100.0	100.0	100.0	100.0	100.0	100.0	100.0	100.0	100.0	100.0	100.0	100.0	100.0
Percent across:													
Institutions (N=299)	6.3	9.4	5.4	21.1	28.1	15.0	22.1	65.2	9.7	1.3	2.7	13.7	100.0
Community non-residential (N=42)	23.8	26.2	23.8	73.8	16.7	0.0	9.5	26.2	0.0	0.0	0.0	0.0	100.0
Community residential (N=72)	23.6	11.1	16.7	51.4	25.0	9.7	9.7	44.4	4.2	0.0	0.0	0.0	100.0
Total (N=413)	11.1	11.4	9.2	31.7	26.4	12.6	18.7	57.7	7.7	1.0	1.9	10.6	100.0

$x^2 = 179.76$, df = 16, $\rho > .999$

TABLE C-3.1

INITIAL PLACEMENT BY SEX

(Row and Column Percentages)

Initial Placement	Sex		Totals (N=416)
	Male (N=315)	Female (N=101)	
Percent down:			
Institution	73.0	65.0	71.2
Community nonresidential	11.0	2.0	8.9
Community residential	16.0	33.0	19.9
Totals	100.0	100.0	100.0
Percent across:			
Institution (N=296)	78.0	22.0	100.0
Community nonresidential (N=37)	95.0	5.0	100.0
Community residential (N=83)	60.0	40.0	100.0
Totals (N=416)	75.7	24.3	100.0

χ^2 = 18.51, df = 2, ρ > .999

TABLE C-3.2.1

INITIAL PLACEMENT BY RACE

(Row and Column Percentages)

Initial Placement	Race		Totals (N=410)
	White (N=171)	Black (N=239)	
Percent down:			
Institution	78.9	65.3	71.2
Community nonresidential	8.2	9.2	8.7
Community residential	12.9	25.5	20.1
Totals	100.0	100.0	100.0
Percent across:			
Institution (N=291)	46.4	53.6	100.0
Community nonresidential (N=36)	38.9	61.1	100.0
Community residential (N=83)	26.5	73.5	100.0
Totals (N=410)	41.7	58.3	100.0

$\chi^2 = 11.47$, df = 4, $.975 < \rho < .999$

TABLE C-3.2.2

INITIAL PLACEMENT BY RACE AND SEX

(Row and Column Percentages)

Initial Placement	WHITE			BLACK			TOTALS (N=410)
	Male (N=130)	Female (N=41)	Totals (N=171)	Male (N=181)	Female (N=58)	Totals (N=239)	
Percent down:							
Institution	76.9	80.5	77.8	71.2	55.2	67.8	72.0
Community nonresidential	10.0	2.4	8.2	12.7	6.9	11.3	10.0
Community residential	13.1	17.1	14.0	15.5	37.9	20.9	18.0
Totals	100.0	100.0	100.0	100.0	100.0	100.0	100.0
Percent across:							
Institution (N=295)	33.9	11.2	45.1	44.1	10.8	54.9	100.0
Community nonresidential (N=41)	31.7	2.4	34.1	56.1	9.8	65.9	100.0
Community residential (N=74)	23.0	9.5	32.5	37.8	29.7	67.5	100.0
Totals (N=410)	31.7	10.0	41.7	44.2	14.1	58.3	100.0

χ^2 = 149.34, df = 6, ρ > .999

TABLE C-3.2.1

INITIAL PLACEMENT BY OFFENSE CLASS

(Row and Column Percentages)

Initial Placement	Offense Class			Totals (N=416)
	Nonaggressive (N=189)	Aggressive and Noninjurious (N=103)	Aggressive and Injurious (N=124)	
Percent down:				
Institutions	67.7	72.8	75.0	71.2
Community non-residential	7.4	9.7	10.5	8.9
Community residential	24.9	17.5	14.5	19.9
Totals	100.0	100.0	100.0	100.0
Percent across:				
Institutions (N=296)	43.3	25.3	31.4	100.0
Community non-residential (N=37)	37.9	27.0	35.1	100.0
Community residential (N=83)	56.6	21.7	21.7	100.0
Totals (N=416)	45.4	24.8	29.8	100.0

χ^2 = 6.46, df = 4, .80 < ρ < .90

TABLE C-3.3.2

INITIAL PLACEMENT BY SEX AND OFFENSE CLASS

(Row and Column Percentages)

INITIAL PLACEMENT	Male				Female				TOTALS (N=405)
	Nonaggressive (N=96)	Aggressive and Noninjurious (N=96)	Aggressive and Injurious (N=112)	Total (N=304)	Nonaggressive (N=87)	Aggressive and Noninjurious (N=4)	Aggressive and Injurious (N=10)	Total (N=101)	
Percent down:									
Institutions[a]	71.9	71.9	75.9	73.4	55.2	75.0	70.0	57.4	69.4
Community non-residential	13.5	2.1	9.8	8.6	1.1	0.0	10.0	2.0	6.9
Community residential	14.6	26.0	14.3	18.0	43.7	25.0	20.0	40.6	23.7
TOTAL	100.0	100.0	100.0	100.0	100.0	100.0	100.0	100.0	100.0
Percent across:									
Institutions (N=281)	24.6	24.6	30.2	79.4	17.1	1.2	2.4	20.6	100.0
Community non-residential (N=28)	46.4	7.1	39.3	92.8	3.6	0.0	3.6	7.2	100.0
Community residential (N=96)	14.6	26.0	16.7	57.3	39.6	1.0	2.1	42.7	100.0
TOTAL	23.7	23.7	27.7	75.1	21.5	1.0	2.4	24.9	100.0

$x^2 = 41.4$, df = 10, $\rho > .999$

[a]Private institutional placements comprise 65.2, 33.3 and 18.8 percent of all institutional placements for nonaggressive, aggressive and noninjurious and aggressive and injurious males, respectively. Total private institutional placements are 37.7 percent of all male institutional placements. In addition, private institutional placements comprise 41.7 percent of all institutional placements for nonaggressive females. No aggressive females were placed in private institutions. Total private institutional placements are 34.5 percent of all female institutional placements. Finally, 37 percent of all institutional placements were made to private institutions.

155

TABLE C-3.4

INITIAL PLACEMENT BY AGE AT FIRST OFFENSE

(Row and Column Percentages)

Initial Placement	Age at First Offense			Totals (N=406)
	< 12.0 (N=126)	12.1-14.0 (N=181)	> 14.1 (N=99)	
Percent down:				
Institution	73.0	72.9	70.7	72.4
Community non-residential	10.3	7.7	13.1	9.9
Community residential	16.7	19.4	16.2	17.7
Totals	100.0	100.0	100.0	100.0
Percent across:				
Institution (N=294)	31.3	44.9	23.8	100.0
Community non-residential (N=40)	32.5	55.0	32.5	100.0
Community residential (N=72)	29.2	48.6	22.2	100.0
Totals (N=406)	31.0	44.6	24.4	100.0

χ^2 = 2.456, df = 4, .50 < ρ > .70

TABLE C-3.5

INITIAL PLACEMENT AND AGE OF ADMISSION

(Row and Column Percentages)

Initial Placement	Age of Admission			Totals (N=406)
	$\leq$ 14.0 (N=129)	14.1-16.0 (N=129)	$\geq$ 16.1 (N=157)	
Percent down:				
Institutions	76.7	71.4	68.8	72.1
Community non-residential	4.7	10.8	14.0	10.1
Community residential	18.6	17.8	17.2	17.8
Totals	100.0	100.0	100.0	100.0
Percent across:				
Institutions (N=299)	33.1	30.8	36.1	100.0
Community non-residential (N=42)	14.3	33.3	52.4	100.0
Community residential (N=47)	32.4	31.1	36.5	100.0
Totals	31.1	31.1	37.8	100.0

χ^2 = 6.95, df = 4, .80 < ρ < .90

TABLE C-3.6

INITIAL PLACEMENT AND DELAY

(Row and Column Percentages)

Initial Placement	Delay			Totals (N=414)
	1-18 months (N=154)	19-36 months (N=145)	37+ months (N=115)	
Percent down:				
Institution	73.4	73.1	68.7	72.0
Community non-residential	8.4	10.3	12.2	10.1
Community residential	18.2	16.6	19.1	17.9
Totals	100.0	100.0	100.0	100.0
Percent across:				
Institution (N=298)	37.9	35.6	26.5	100.0
Community non-residential (N=42)	31.0	35.7	33.3	100.0
Community residential (N=74)	37.8	32.4	29.8	100.0
Totals (N=414)	37.2	35.0	27.8	100.0

$\chi^2 = 1.37$, df = 4, .80 < ρ < .90

Reports published by Michigan Department of Social Services are designed to analyze and describe a wide variety of issues in the areas of public welfare policy and allied subjects. A price is listed for those publications for which there is a charge.

LIST OF PUBLICATIONS ISSUED OR FORTHCOMING

Studies in Welfare Policy, Number 1
The Employment of AFDC Recipients in Michigan,
by Vernon K. Smith and Aydin Ulusan, June, 1972

Rising Medical Costs in Michigan: The Scope of
the Problem and the Effectiveness of Current
Controls. Report of the Technical Work Group
on Health Care Costs, by Bruce Stuart and Bruce
Spitz, July, 1973. $5.00

The Decentralization Project: Year-End Research
and Evaluation Report on the Effectiveness of
Treatment in Institutional and Community-Based
Juvenile Delinquency Facilities, by Laurence J.
Max, November, 1973

Studies in Welfare Policy, Number 2
Welfare Work Incentives: The Earnings Exemption
and Its Impact Upon AFDC Employment, Earnings,
and Program Costs, by Vernon K. Smith,
November, 1974. $5.00

Studies in Welfare Policy, Number 3
Utilization of the 1973 Michigan Property Tax
Credit by Welfare Recipients, by Robert W.
Swanson, April, 1975